Ex...

SPORTS

Be the Best at Sports, Business & Life with NLP Neuro Linguistic Programming

Jimmy Petruzzi

Excel at Sports

Be the Best in Sports, Business and Life with NLP Neuro Linguistic Programming

© 2011 Jimmy Petruzzi

ISBN 978-1-873483-44-2
First Edition

Published by
DragonRising Publishing
The Starfields Network Ltd.
45 Gildredge Road
Eastbourne
East Sussex
BN21 4RY
United Kingdom
www.DragonRising.com

Printed and bound in Great Britain by
CPI Antony Rowe, Chippenham and Eastbourne

Excel at SPORTS

Be the Best in Sports, Business & Life with NLP Neuro Linguistic Programming

Dedication

To Nieve, Dario, my sisters, my cousin Tony, Aunty, Uncle, and my closest family and friends who are my inspiration and have always supported my dreams.

To my partner, Sara Lou-Ann Jones, who continues to support and encourage my dreams and ambitions.

Thank you.

Praise for Excel at Sports

You need look no further than Jim's book, *Excel at Sports*, when it comes to succeeding in sports or life. Jim shows you that anything is possible if you stay focused and motivated.

Andy Paschalidis, Presenter
Sky Sports Radio Australia

This book is excellent. Throughout my 18-year playing career as a professional footballer I used all the techniques mentioned. This is something that came naturally to me and had a big effect on my journey-playing professional sport. I often used the disappointments and setbacks, of which there are many along the way (as all athletes will testify), in a positive manner to drive me on and to achieve my goals.

For those people who are not fortunate enough to have the natural gift and don't find it easy to get self motivated, the various practical exercises explained in this book will be invaluable, not only to athletes but to anyone who have goals and ambitions and want to be the achievers in life.

Andy Hill, Former Professional Footballer
Manchester United FC, 1981–1984
Bury FC, 1984–1989
Mancehster City FC, 1989–1995
Port Vale FC, 1995–1998

An excellent book! I highly recommend it to any coach looking to get the best out of his team. Jim has been a big part of the success of several teams I have coached.

David Dias, Former Professional Footballer
Angolan National Football Team

I would highly recommend that any coach or sports person get a copy of Jim's new book, *Excel at Sports*.

Paul Trinci Lynne

Praise for Jimmy Petruzzi

I found [Jim's] course very informative. It's an absolute must if you're looking to gain the edge that just might make the difference.

Dr. Tony Strudwick, Sports Scientist
Manchester United

Jim Petruzzi is the perfect example of someone who, through hard work, passion, perseverance, study and practical experience, has achieved significant status as a professional football conditioning coach and sport psychologist. Having worked closely with Jim before, I can honestly say he is one of the very best in the world at what he does. I wish him all the very best in the future.

Nathan Hall, 1st Team Coach and Head of Human Performance
Thai Port FC

Jimmy Petruzzi is one of the best-qualified coaches of his kind in the world. He has worked with several top teams including West Ham and Crystal Palace and his advanced training methods pay dividends on the pitch.

The lads [at Bury FC] took to him and showed belief in his methods. His work is structured and the results are a long-term thing.

Chris Casper, Former Manager
Bury FC
In an interview with the Bury Times

Jimmy was an important part of turning around our season and his scientific approach to things like psychology has been a revelation to us.

In recent seasons the likes of Dave Nugent, Colin Kazim-Richards, Simon Whaley and Tom Kennedy have all come through the youth system to make an impact in the first team and go on to play for Championship clubs and England U21. The strength of the Bury Youth System is something Jim must take credit for.

Ross Johnson, Former Director
Bury FC

My son, Jordan, visits Jim once a year for a 6 week course. He has been going to see Jim since he was 14.

He has always been a talented footballer, but he needed something extra to help him achieve his football goals.

I can say that the time he has spent with Jim has changed my son's life, both on and off the football field, with all the help and advise Jim has given him, both physically and mentally.

My son now has a 2-year professional football contract and visits Jim every year for top up sessions.

We can't thank Jim enough for everything he has done to help Jordan achieve his goals. I don't think my son would be where he is today if we had not met Jim.

Paul Trinci Lynne

Contents

As an athlete, you can't dictate certain elements of the game such as the weather, refereeing decisions, the opposition, or performing. You can only focus on yourselves and play the card you're dealt.

You need to create a new balance when you're stuck out-of-form, but amid the pressure and anxiety we all face in sports, it can be difficult. Start making changes by asking yourself what you want to achieve and how you would like to perform. Then, begin to focus on the positive, not the negative.

Imprint self-belief in your identity. The key to self-belief and your identity is creating a sense of purpose and aligning them with your goals. Each of us has an identity and a set of values and beliefs which affect our performance in sports. Find out your self-belief and get on the path of success.

One of the most important things in sports is to dream. Every successful sports person talks about The Dream. Rediscover and ignite your dreams.

Dreams will only ever be dreams if they are left in the shelves of our mind. The underpinning of any sports person's success is setting goals. If you're not driving your own bus, then you can be sure someone else will drive it for you. Having set goals helps you stay the course through thick and thin.

Chapter 13: Relaxation, 67

Imagine living in a world without modern technology. Whilst there are many benefits to modern technology, the one thing we are probably all guilty of is not giving ourselves the opportunity to unwind.

Chapter 14: Power of Visualisation and Imagery, 73

Athletes use visualisation to focus on how they want the outcome of a competition or training session to go. This helps the athlete stay relaxed, focused and confident.

Chapter 15: Proximity, 90

Your network is your net worth. Make sure you associate and practice with people who are going to have a positive effect on you and your team.

Chapter 16: Laughter, 92

Sports can be very challenging and demanding. It is easy to get wrapped up in emotion during competition. The power of a good sense of humour can lighten up and freshen the situation.

Chapter 17: Part I—Letting Go of the Past, 94

The one thing for certain in sports, as in life, is that no one knows how long they have. If you knew how long your career was going to be, what would you do differently?

Chapter 17: Part II—The Path We Take, 99

Imagine yourself standing at a crossroad of your career in sports. You have come to a decision point. Do you continue to do walk along the same path or do you make new pathways for your career?

Conclusion, 102

About the Author, 103

Other Books from DragonRising Publishing, 105

Acknowledgements

I would like to take this opportunity to thank all of my colleagues, clients, and students who have contributed to this book.

I would especially like to thank Andy Paschalidis, Dr Tony Strudwick, Mark Hughes, Wyatt Woodsmall, Carlos Alberto Da Luz, Chris Casper, all the boys at Sky Sports radio, Chris Butler, the guys at City Talk FM, BBC Radio, BBC GMR, Ang, Andy Hill, David Dias, Lee Murphy, Colin Kazeem Richards, Tony Basha, Welsh Girls Lacrosse team, the lads at Bury football club 2003 to 2006, Jeremy Lazarus, Ross Johnson, the lads at Accrington Stanley, Brent Peters. The Mind–Body–Spirit team, the guys at Treelife and everyone who ever supported my work.

Special thanks to my editor, Sheryl, and to everyone at DragonRising Publishing for believing in me.

Preface

*"We are all ordinary people, though ordinary people can sometimes do
extraordinary things by shining a light in a dark room."*

*"The winners in life think constantly in terms of I can, I will, and I am.
Losers, on the other hand, concentrate their waking thoughts on what
they should have or would have done, or what they can't do."*

—Denis Waitley

Many elite athletes and sports people say the mental aspects of competing in a
sport make the difference between being a champion or not. In these pages
you will find insights into the skills, principles and mindsets that many of the world's
best athletes and sports people use to be at the top of their game and to fulfil their
potential.

This book is full of practical exercises on how to use your mind more effectively,
to gain more success in sports as a participant, get the best out of yourself as a coach,
or get the best out of your players as a coach.

It provides coaches, PE teachers, trainers, and football players the techniques
and strategies they can use to enhance their ability as a coach or player.

These techniques focus on achieving results. If you're serious about achieving
results, this book is for you. It will help you get more consistent results and the best
out of yourself, whether you are a player aspiring to fulfil your physical potential, a
coach, trainer, or teacher who wants to get the best out of your team, or whether you're
involved with an amateur or pro team.

This book is designed so you can use the content over and over again. You can
return to the book to help you to get the best out of yourself and your athletes.

USING NLP IN SPORTS

Neuro Linguistic Programming (NLP) is the process of creating models of excellence.
Modelling is the complex activity of capturing—in learnable, transferable code—the
mental skills that make the difference between an excellent performer and an average
performer, between an excellent athlete and an average one, between a person who
is motivated to get the best out of themselves in training and one who is not. NLP,

then, is the process of identifying, coding and transferring precisely those differences in a learnable form so that interested participants and companies can significantly upgrade their performance to new levels of excellence.

Results in sports depend crucially on your ability to use your mind effectively. Many elite athletes know there is as little as a 1% difference between the person who is ranked 1st and the person who is ranked 50th in the world! They know the mental aspects they use in their sport make the difference between being a champion or not. Whether you are a teacher or a fitness professional, and at whatever level of your sport you compete or coach, your mindset has a major influence on the degree of success and fulfilment you achieve.

This book gives helps you improve your mindset by implementing techniques and strategies, such as:

- being able to create excellent states of mind at will, regardless of circumstances,
- learning how to instil confidence and motivation in yourself and others,
- communicating more powerfully and effectively,
- using positive language and positive instructions when coaching or teaching, or when giving a halftime team talk,
- anchoring, or focusing, on past positive experiences in a sensory manner so as to recreate future success,
- developing a cue which will enable you or an athlete to tap into a state of mind; i.e., confidence, relaxation, motivation,
- developing outcome setting so that aims are planned and agreed on that maintain and increase motivation, and
- learning "reframing" so that all experiences and performances are viewed from a positive perspective with success being internalised to the performer or team.

All these methods can be easily incorporated into the practical arena without hours spent in the class room.

Many people study NLP to help them become more effective in their chosen field, for their own personal development, or for becoming more confident and motivated. NLP patterns can be employed across a wide range of applications, from fields as diverse as business, sports, education, team building, sales, marketing, personal development, leadership, and coaching. NLP techniques provide people with the opportunity to grow and develop, helping them to fulfil their potential and be the best they can be. NLP can be used to develop and enhance performance.

NLP is about creating models of success. The most important thing is finding role models that will allow you to create success. This could be anything from a behavioural pattern, characteristic, technique, or skill such as confidence, motivation, a technique or skill, to modelling a skilled sport participant such as David Beckham's free kick technique. Another powerful direction might be about finding athletes that truly participate in their sport in an exceptional way and understanding how they do it; e.g., Lance Armstrong's dedication and determination.

Imagine a situation where you can sit down and talk to a true role model of success. What goes through the mind of a true champion such as Federer or Tiger Woods? Exactly how do they run their brains to create that success? If you know that, you could take that information and instil it in yourself and others. This is what NLP is really about.

NLP modelling is the art of identifying, eliciting, and transferring the set of differences present in someone who excels at a given activity compared and someone who is mediocre at the same activity even when they have similar skills. NLP modelling is by far the highest skill level in NLP and can be used to capture patterns of excellence present in anyone in any context.

This book is full of practical exercises on how to use your mind more effectively by emulating the mindset of champions and by using techniques from NLP, hypnotherapy, and other psychological strategies to gain more success in sports to consistently get the best out of yourself and others.

I have also included several real-life sports stories based on my experience in working with people across a broad range of sports linked to these techniques and strategies. This will help you understand the applications of the techniques so that you can use them to build an association of them to your own experiences.

If you're serious about fulfilling your potential and achieving results, this book is for you.

Anything is possible in sports. This book can help you discover your potential and reach your dreams. You don't need to settle for anything less than what you want or what you want to be.

We are all special and have a lot to offer, but sometimes we all need a little advice, support, or an objective viewpoint. With my coaching experience I know how to help people create a fulfilling life. This book is best used as a guide to help you make the most out of your ability as an athlete and to create and make the most out of your opportunities. It works at the deepest level of your mind and offers techniques that athletes use to get world class results

This is a how-to book. It is easy to follow and has step-by-step instructions and examples you can relate to. In fact, to use an analogy, think of a satellite navigation system in a car. How many people are interested in the complexity of how the system works? How important and useful is it for them to know how it works? The most important thing for the consumer is knowing where they want to go and how to programme the system.

Imagine your mind is similar to a satellite navigation system and the tools in this book are a set of instructions that assist you to programme your mind to help you achieve the results you want in life.

IT'S THE JOURNEY THAT MAKES THE DESTINATION SPECIAL

If climbing Mount Everest was easy, it wouldn't be such a beautiful experience. Sports are about challenges. It's not always easy. We have to roll up our sleeves and get busy when faced with challenges. When we make it to the other side of our difficulties and we look in the mirror, we see our truth. We know what we are capable of and challenges get fewer and farther apart as we develop our confidence through realizing our capabilities.

The Making of a Champion

There are many "impossible" success stories. Michael Jordan, one of the world's most accomplished basketball players, didn't make his high school basketball team.

In 2001, Natalie Du Toit was riding her motor scooter when she was hit by a careless driver. She lost her left leg just above the knee. Less than 2 years later she qualified for the finals of the 800-meter freestyle swimming event at the 2002 Commonwealth Games. In 2008, Natalie qualified for both the Paralympic and Olympic games.

In March of 2007, Randy Couture came out of retirement at age 43 and challenged 27-year-old Big Tim Sylvia for the UFC heavyweight title. The insiders of mixed martial arts not only thought Randy didn't have a chance to win, but that he would get seriously hurt in the process. The result: Randy almost knocked out Big Tim eight seconds into the fight and completely dominated him for all 5 rounds. It gives hope to all 30-, 40-, and 50-year-old fitness wannabes, doesn't it?

In 2003, Bethany was attacked by a 14-foot tiger shark, which ripped off her left arm just below the shoulder. By the time she reached the hospital, she had lost 70% of her blood. She was surfing 3 weeks later and in 2004, received an ESPY award for Best Comeback Athlete of the Year.

In 1996, Lance Armstrong was diagnosed with testicular cancer. Doctors told him he had a 10% chance of survival. Lance not only survived, but went on to win seven consecutive Tour de France titles, the last in 2005.

Definition of NLP

Neuro: The nervous system (the mind), through which our experiences are processed via the five senses:

+ visual (sight),
+ auditory (hearing),
+ kinaesthetic (feeling),
+ olfactory (smell), and
+ gustatory (taste).

Linguistic: Language and other nonverbal communication systems through which our neural representations are coded, ordered and given meaning. Includes:

+ pictures,
+ sounds,
+ feelings,
+ tastes,
+ smells, and
+ words (self talk)

Programming: The ability to discover and utilize the programs that we run in our neurological systems (in our communications to ourselves and others) to achieve our specific and desired outcomes.

In other words, NLP is how to use the language of the mind to achieve specific and desired outcomes and improve results.

NLP has three key benefits:

1. improving communication,
2. changing behaviours and beliefs, and
3. modelling excellence.

NLP is based on principles that are very different from traditional psychology. While traditional clinical psychology is primarily concerned with describing difficulties, categorising them, and searching for historical causes, NLP is interested in how our thoughts, actions, and feelings work together to produce our experiences. Founded on the modern sciences of biology, linguistics, and information, NLP begins with new principles of how the mind/brain works.

If It's Not Working, Change What You're Doing

Our specific thoughts, actions, and feelings consistently produce specific results. We may be happy or unhappy with these results. If we repeat the same thoughts, actions, and feelings, we'll get the same results. The process works perfectly. If we want to change our results, then we need to change the thoughts, actions, and feelings that go into producing them. Once we understand specifically how we create and maintain our inner thoughts and feelings, it is a simple matter for us to change them to more useful ones and to teach them to others. As well as using a winning mindset throughout the book, we will use techniques which are derived from NLP and human excellence.

Chapter 1

Taking Responsibility

"You have no control over what the other guy does.
You only have control over what you do."

—A.J. Kitt

I remember watching the Wimbledon tennis semi-final in 2000. Tim Henman was playing Goran Ivanisevic. Henman was in a strong position and looked likely to win and make the final. Rain interrupted the match and the players went off. After the rain interval, Henman seemed to have lost his momentum and Ivanisevic took the initiative and went on to win the match. During an interview after the match, Henman alluded that the break in play was a potential factor in losing his rhythm and the match.

Was the break in play an important factor? I am sure it was, though it was a break in play for both players. One used it as an opportunity to refocus. The other would end up using it as a potential excuse.

I am sure you have heard the saying, "If you get lemons, make lemonade."

Sometimes things don't go the way we want them to. It's during these times we need to be focused and make the most of every situation.

VICTIM THINKING

In sports, athletes, managers, and coaches can have a tendency to blame the referee, the weather, the pitch, everything else other than looking within themselves. The belief that "they" cause our feelings begins at a young age, is confirmed throughout our teenage years, and becomes our unquestioned reality by adulthood. The referees don't like us, we can't win away, those fans get on my nerves, my coach stresses me, the club doesn't look after me, and they're ruining our team!

Our aim is to become aware of how we respond to outside circumstances and to exercise more choice in our responses. If somebody typically "makes" us feel good, we choose to accept and thoroughly enjoy this. If somebody else typically "makes" us feel

> Two long-time golfers were standing overlooking the river getting ready to hit their shots. One golfer looked at the other and said, "Look at those idiots fishing in the rain."

upset or irritable, we choose to cease cooperating with them. In essence, our aim is to develop our ability to "drive our own bus" instead of being passive passengers.

Victim or Not Victim

Do you make excuses or are always looking for people to blame for your circumstances? Do you do the running and take control of the situation? Do you become empowered and stronger than you were before?

In NLP we talk about people living either *at effect* or *at cause*. If you are *at effect*, you may blame others or circumstances for your bad moods, for what you have not achieved, or for your life in general. You may feel powerless or depend on others in order for you to feel good about yourself or about life. You may think, "If only my coach–manager–teammates–parents understood me and helped me achieve my dreams or did what I wanted or what is best for me, then life would be great."

If you wait and hope for others to provide what you think you need, then you are *at effect*, or a victim of circumstances. How much fun is that? How much fun do you think it is for others to be around you? Believing that someone else is responsible or making them responsible for your happiness or mood is very limiting and gives this person some mystical power over you. This can cause you a great deal of anguish.

Those who live their lives *at effect* often see themselves or live their lives as victims with no choices whatsoever. The irony is that they do have choices, but they have chosen not to choose and instead are responsive to whatever is given to them.

Being *at cause* means that when you have choices in your life, you choose what is best for you while also ensuring the choice is ecological for those around you— those in your community and your society. Sometimes you go so far as to consider the consequences of your actions on others while not taking into consideration your emotional well-being. Believing you are responsible for the emotional well-being of someone else places a heavy burden on you and can cause a great deal of stress.

Exercise

+ List three areas of your life where you're living *at effect* and would like to change; e.g., my teammates are making me unhappy, I can never play well away from home, etc.
+ List three areas of your life where you are living *at cause* within your sports environment; e.g., where you do the running.

By changing your attitude and accepting responsibility, you feel more empowered and in control. One of the exercises I do with my clients is the Responsibility Contract. This helps to put them in the drivers' seat.

Responsibility Contract

I hereby take full responsibility for my life from today onwards.

You can either live your life *at effect* or *at cause*. True winners live *at cause* and take responsibility. Under some of the most difficult circumstances, they turn things around to their advantage. Life is about looking at the big picture. It is easy to lose track of the big picture.

_____

Your signature

The Choice is Yours

Life isn't always fair. How else do you explain some of the injustices of this world? However, whatever the situation in your life and at whatever point you are, you can turn things around.

I think we all go through times when we question certain things—poor referee decisions, the manager's tactics, our team, our family and even ourselves. I don't profess to know all the answers, or any answers, for that matter. However, life is short and all in all does anyone really know the meaning of it all?

What does anyone know about anything other than what are told or what we read?

The only thing that is certain is that we are only on this planet in our present form for a short time. We owe it to ourselves to make the most of every situation and every millisecond.

Life can be very challenging and we all have a story to tell. Some people tend to tell it more than others. They dwell in the past and spend a lifetime going over the same problems and stories, but never do anything to change it. Sometimes you don't get dealt the best cards in life, but you do have a choice in how you respond. It is within your responses that your life is shaped.

Chapter 2

Breaking Bad Habits

"Bad habits are easier to abandon today than tomorrow".

Yiddish Proverb

Do you ever find yourself hitting your golf swing at the golf range really well? During practise, do you hit your tennis backhand really well? Do you easily score goals in training? But, when it comes to a match situation, do you struggle to perform?

Do you find it really hard to grasp a technique or a skill; it just won't sink in? Do you find yourself repeating certain types of behaviour over and over again? One that once you have repeated the behaviour, you think, "Damn, I can't believe I did that. I can't believe I did it again."

All of us have habits. Some of them serve us and some of them can be detrimental and self destructive to us and the people around us. Do you have any habits you would like to change? Are there certain things you do that you are fed up doing and have reached the point you want to kick that habit? Perhaps it's faltering under pressure or letting the fear of failure ruin your game. Perhaps it's a technical error such as fluffing a kick on the football, slicing a golf swing, or messing up your tennis serve.

Once a habitual behaviour has been learnt, it can be beneficial for positive behaviours—exercising or training hard, focusing on key moments in a match, or having confidence in your ability, or it can be detrimental for negative behaviours—messing up a golf swing under pressure, doubting your ability, or not performing your best. Habits can reinforce a negative behaviour, such as fear and complacency, and can sabotage your sports performance and cause you to live within your self-conceived limitations.

The good news is that, providing you want to remove an existing habit, it is possible to remove it very quickly. If you are training an athlete or you are an athlete who is struggling to perform a technique, struggling with confidence, or generally trying to stay motivated, NLP can be an effective, quick, and easy way to build a strong motivation for a desired behaviour. It is also more likely to produce a lasting change.

Consciously, we can distinguish between a good or bad habit. Most people know how to perform technically and tactically in their sport and know what foods are good for them. So, why is it that people carry on sabotaging their lives by smoking, drinking, and feeling negative? Why don't they change? Because they are dealing with habitual behaviour and they don't know how to break it.

Habitual behaviour is typically a way of creating order or structure in day-to-day life. First, it is learnt and then becomes automatic without the person being consciously aware of doing it. Negative habitual behaviours, such as smoking and drinking, can last a lifetime and can be detrimental to a person's physical and mental health.

Let's explore the mind, which is where all habits start.

The mind has two parts: the conscious and the subconscious. A useful analogy is an iceberg. The conscious mind is the little bit that sticks out of the water. The subconscious mind is the huge bit hidden away underneath the surface.

The subconscious is where all the things you have learnt to do without thinking about them are located.

For instance, when you first drove a car, you had to consciously work out where to put each foot and how to use each new control. As your driving skills developed, you handed more and more control over to your subconscious mind. Now you are so proficient that you can drive, navigate, and talk to your passenger, all at the same time!

It is the subconscious mind that is in control of our behaviour most of the time. This is the reason why people find it very difficult to stop smoking—even though they may consciously decide that smoking is bad for their health, costs a fortune, is ruining their complexion, etc., they have not taken into account their subconscious reasons for wanting to carry on smoking. Go back to the iceberg analogy. If the little bit at the top wants to go one way and the huge bit at the bottom wants to go the other way, guess who's going to win?

The conscious mind can only handle a limited amount of information at any given time. Have you ever seen someone trying to drive, talk on their mobile phone, and put on makeup at the same time, and they are not doing any of them very well? That's because the conscious mind is overwhelmed with information.

The unconscious mind, on the other hand, is aware of everything that is going on—the sound of the cars outside, the breeze blowing through the window, the sound of the TV in the background, your feet landing against the pavement as you walk, the aeroplane flying overhead, the millions of memories we store in your mind from the day you were born, birthdays, scoring that winning goal, your first kiss. Everything.

Once you understand about the role of the subconscious mind, you can understand where a lot of odd behaviour comes from. People get stuck in a rut because their subconscious doesn't know how to change. People can get disturbing thoughts or feelings they don't understand because the subconscious thinks that something bad is about to happen.

OUR BEHAVIOURS

Our behaviours and body are governed by our subconscious mind. We do not need to tell our finger nails to grow. We do not need to tell our hair to grow, our heart to beat, or tell ourselves to breathe. When we are hungry we do not need to consciously tell ourselves how to do it. If we are thirsty, we do not need to consciously tell ourselves how to make a cup of tea.

We do it like we are on auto pilot—subconsciously.

Successful people, whether they are top athletes or entrepreneurs, have mastered the combined power of their conscious and subconscious minds to produce success. Many of the rest of us haven't tapped into the unlimited potential of our minds because we lack the understanding of how our minds actually work. When we focus our effort on creating unity with the conscious and subconscious minds, we can achieve a greater sense of happiness and success in our lives than we ever thought possible.

That explains why people make conscious decisions at the start of every January to go to the gym and get into shape, only to give up by February. Statistics say 90 percent of people who join a gym give up in first six months. We have all the right intentions, but the subconscious mind steers us away.

In order for behaviour to make a change and last, we must work at a subconscious level. If we are going to give up cigarettes and stay off them, we need to change at a subconscious level. "How?" you ask. "How can I give up chocolate, give up smoking, stop biting my nails, or stop sabotaging my success?" By using the New Behaviour Generator.

The New Behaviour Generator is one of NLP's simplest and most powerful patterns for changing behaviour. Use it to

+ increase confidence,

+ instil motivation,

+ get rid of anger problems,

+ break habits,

+ improve technical skills,

+ increase performance,

+ overcome fears and anxieties, and

+ improve tactical awareness.

You see, the subconscious mind needs clear directions in a very specific format if it's going to motivate you to do something. Without this "roadmap," change can be very difficult. With this powerful technique, the new behaviour is easy and automatic. Old habits you want to get rid of fall away; new healthy habits you wish to replace them with take their place. One of the things to keep in mind with this technique is that by changing your state of mind—the state of mind you're in when you make mistakes are under pressure, lose focus, make tactical and technical errors—you can change your state of mind from a negative one to a more positive one. When you are in a more positive state of mind, you achieve a more positive outcome.

For example, you may link feeling nervous in a certain situation in a match to the way the play is going and you begin to make technical errors. NLP helps you to change your state of mind from feeling nervous to feeling empowered. The new state of mind produces a new outcome. Instead of making technical errors, in your new empowered state you feel more confident and take the initiative.

To achieve this new state of mind, use the two techniques of the New Behaviour Generator to assist you or an athlete you are coaching in overcoming negative behaviour and unwanted bad habits.

Technique 1: Helping an Athlete

By working through Technique 1, you can assist an athlete to alter their perspective on difficult exercises in their training schedule and limiting beliefs that could be stunting their progress towards their performance goals.

When I was working with a youth team at the Bury football club, one of the key factors in successfully helping the players to not only fulfil their potential, but to believe they could become professional players and play at the highest level, was to change the way they thought of themselves so they were no longer just players for Bury. I had them learn what the psychological thought processes of elite players were. We achieved this by doing techniques similar to those in the following list, both passively in conversation and in structured exercises. The result of producing a mental winning environment was immense and we went on to break the national average of youth players who turned professional.

1. Identify a technique or resource, such as confidence, that an athlete would like to have. It should be a technique or resource that an athlete understands is an important part of their training schedule. It can even be something they don't necessarily enjoy, such as passing a ball, being more confident, or developing a skill.

2. Ask an athlete to imagine a time when they successfully completed the technique. Ask them to recreate the positive feelings they received from doing so. Now ask them to go back into the experience and recreate what they felt, saw, and heard, and what it was like.

3. Ask an athlete to imagine themselves in the future having just completed the technique successfully, and then to look at themselves after they have actually done it. Get them to notice the benefits of having done it and to think about the results that will arise from it.

4. Then, ask an athlete to think of themselves doing the technique or skill easily and enjoyably in the future. Every time they think of the technique or skill, they get a good feeling of anticipation and hear positive, encouraging internal voices. Ask them to see how good that "future you" feels about the progress they're making. Have them imagine having a sense of joy and pleasure at having successfully completed the technique or skill and enjoying the benefits.

5. Ask an athlete whether they are happy with the change. If the answer is yes, repeat steps 3 and 4 again while fine-tuning the benefits.

6. Identify when an athlete is next going to do the technique in a game. Get them to imagine themselves doing it, easily and enjoyably.

Technique 2: Helping You to Develop a New Behaviour

Building new pathways in the mind is a great way to adopt a new behaviour. I call it repatterning existing negative thought processes and replacing them with a more productive level of thinking. Doing this powerful mental technique can be enough to move yourself forward into a more productive thought process and outcome.

Teach your players to replicate the thought processes of elite players and it will help them be winners, not only on the field, but throughout their lives.

First, choose a behaviour you would like to change and decide on a new behaviour to replace it.

1. Either think of a time you demonstrated the behaviour you would like or choose a role model that has the behaviour, skills or abilities that you want for yourself. It could be someone who exhibits confidence or outstanding motivation, or someone who is an excellent public speaker or leader.

2. Close your eyes and visualise yourself or that person in action. Watch it like a movie in your mind. See how you (or the person) look, how you (or the person) use your body. Notice the body posture; what happens during standing, walking, and sitting. Pay close attention. Hear how you (or the person) talk, what you (or the person) say, and how it is being said.

3. Ask yourself, "Do I really want to adopt this behaviour or change the old one?" Confirm that it is what you want for yourself.

4. If you were using a role model, remove them from the visualisation and step into their place. Watch yourself act as the role model did. You have taken over and are acting exactly like your role model. See yourself exhibiting this new behaviour or imagine reliving a time when you exhibited the preferred behaviour.

5. Do you feel any negativity when you watch this movie of yourself? Any doubts that you are capable of producing the new behaviour? Go through the steps again and adjust them, or adjust your action in the movie, until you are happy with what you see and hear in this new behaviour. Feel positive and confident in your abilities.

6. Now, mentally step inside the movie. You are no longer watching yourself but are now inside the movie looking through your own eyes. You are doing the new behaviour just as you did it when you were watching the movie. How does it feel to perform this new behaviour? How does your body feel? How is your posture? What do you hear? How does your voice sound to you?

7. Imagine a future situation where you want to behave this way. Put yourself there. Look through your own eyes at this situation. You are the star of this movie and you are behaving in the new way! Is it all working? Do you need to make any adjustments? If so, start the movie over and tweak the action.

8. Open your eyes and return to the present moment.

9. Imagine that you are now the new you with the new behaviour. Get up and walk around as the new model. Walk the walk and talk the talk. How does it feel?

Chapter 3

Realigning Yourself

"Effort within the mind further limits the mind, because effort implies struggle towards a goal and when you have a goal, a purpose, an end in view, you have placed a limit on the mind."

—Bruce Lee

When I was working at the Bury football club as a performance coach, I used to bring in students from university for work experience who had aspirations of working in football and had ideas of what it would be like. They had built mental images of rubbing shoulders with some of the top football stars, owning fast cars, living in mansions, dating glamorous women, having loads of money, and all on a few hours work a day.

I would take the students through the "week in the life" of working in the coaching department of a football club. By the end of the week, most of their perceptions had completely changed. It was sure different to what they had built up! It was really hard work and little or no glamour. That said, occasionally there was a student that really enjoyed the week and pursued a career in football.

One student worked with me for more than a week. One very demanding week in which we lost a couple of games and the general atmosphere was tense. Getting up early and finishing late had started to make the student a bit tired. I asked the student halfway through the week what he thought. He said he was enjoying it, but the whole thing was a bit more demanding than he thought it would be. He was also in the midst of his final dissertation at university and it was keeping him up until the all hours of the night. But he said that if he did the hard work now, things were sure to get easier in the future.

In his own words, he gave me a Muhammad Ali quote in regards to working hard now would make things easier later. I thought, "Right. After you finish your university course, everything is smooth sailing. As easy as that."

> The information in this chapter will help you to get to the bottom of who you are, to understand your inner strengths, and cement the relationship you have with your sport when you're at your best.

There are a seemingly endless number of books, DVDs, CDs, motivational speakers, conferences and courses, and programmes, by coaches on sports psychology and sports performance on the market. There are many people that maintain they have the answers to the problems athletes and coaches face. But, you could be excused for thinking nothing seems to change when you pick up a paper or watch TV.

You might be a member of a team and you have read all the books. You may even have improved your performance for a game or two, maybe even a few games, but then "bang," you're back to where you were.

One day we started at 8 a.m. and ended at 9 p.m. I dropped the student off at his bus stop. He was dragging after a long week of helping me with different duties.

Saturday was match day. Match days are full of excitement and anticipation; after all, it's what we prepare for all week. My student came in to report for his duties looking far from enthusiastic after a long week. As the day progressed it was obvious the game was not going according to plan. We were losing. The manager was not happy, to say the least, and emotions were running high. I asked the student if he would fill the ice baths in the change room so they would be ready for the players after the match. He went off to the change room, which was made up of three rooms—the player's changing area, cubicles, and a spare room for the ice baths.

There was a silence in the change room as the players walked in after their defeat; silence until we could hear someone trying to get out of the spare room. The manager stomped over to the door and flung it open. He roared, "Who in the world is this?" Of course it was the student, who had locked himself in the spare room whilst preparing the ice baths.

The student sidled towards the exit, but the manager bellowed that no one was to leave the change room. The student sat hunched on the bench for the end of match discussion, which was so emotionally charged the air crackled.

When all had settled down and I was driving the student to his stop, I asked him if all was well. He said it was fine; it had been a good week. A Sunday morning training session had been planned in order for the team to prepare for a game on Tuesday. I asked the student if he was going to report. He said, no, he didn't think football was for him. He wanted to get into teaching.

This is when it dawned on me that some people like the idea of doing something, though not the doing; they like what they think doing something might bring to their life, but are not willing to experience the purpose, enjoyment and fulfilment that comes from the hard work necessary to achieve that goal. I would go so far as to guarantee that David Beckham would still be playing football for a Sunday league team if he had not have been so fortunate as to be gracing the field for one of the greatest teams in the world enabling him to align himself with his goals.

LOGICAL LEVELS

An excellent way to align your participation in a sport and identify the exact area you need to work on in your game is by using Logical Levels. Logical Levels give you an understanding of yourself and other people and can help to identify the exact area of your life to work on in order to achieve long-lasting consistency. They can help you to align yourself with your goals and turn the game or team around in the direction you want to go.

Without Logical Levels, it would be like a ship leaving one port for another with no compass, or a plane flying from one destination to another with no navigation system. You could be searching and seeking for this port or destination all your life and yet never find them. You would be just drifting in the abyss. Logical Levels help you find your path and stay on course.

Before we start with the Logical Levels that apply to your participation in your sport—or any goal you may have—let's run the concept and its application to gain an understanding of how they work.

Follow the sequence below and map it according to your participation in your sport; i.e., coach, trainer, athlete, etc. You can reflect on the answers at the end of the chapter when you have a better understanding of Logical Levels.

I did this exercise with the Welsh Women's youth world cup team in conversations with members of the team to help determine which performers already brought the Logical Levels into the ethos of the team. For the team to succeed consistently, we needed all of the team to pull together. I was not trying to clone personalities, but to inspire the players with the importance that everyone needed to buy into the philosophy of success and team unity.

Time to get a pen and paper out and answer the questions in the table below.

The Six Logical Levels

	Level	Questions corresponding to Logical Levels
1	Spirituality and Purpose (This can be viewed as your connection to a wider purpose.)	What is your sense of purpose on an individual level? Why are you participating in your sport? What is your sense of purpose in your sport? Why do you do what you do in your athlete/coach position? What does participating in your sport mean to you?

Level	Questions corresponding to Logical Levels
2 Identity and Mission	Who are you as an individual in your role within your sport? Who are you to different people, such as other players, participants, coaches? Who are you professionally? Are you achieving your purpose? How do you think of yourself on a personal level; i.e., are you enjoying your participation? How do you think of yourself on a professional level; i.e., what are your strengths in your role? Are they tactical, technical, intelligence?
3 Beliefs and Values	Why do you participate in your sport on a personal level? Why do you participate in your sport on a professional level? What do you believe about your personal and professional ability to perform your role within your sport? What are your personal and professional key values? (For example, from a personal perspective, you may believe you are an excellent coach or you may value honesty. From a professional perspective, you may value a high work ethic in training and a 100% commitment from all of your players.)
4 Capabilities and Strategies	How do you go about doing things personally and professionally as a coach and or an athlete? What are your personal and professional capabilities, skills, strategies or action plans?
5 Behaviours	What are your personal and professional behaviours?
6 Environment	Where, when and with who do you display your personal and professional behaviours? What are the external influences on you?

Level 6—Environment: To gain an appreciation of how these Logical Levels work, assume it is 3 p.m. on a Saturday afternoon and you are with your teammates at your home ground ready for a match.

Level 5—Behaviours: You find out you have been left out of the team and you're not sure why. Some of your possible courses of action are (1) go up to coach and ask why, (2) tell one of your teammates how the coach has got it wrong, or (3) start shouting and acting silly with the hope you will grab the coach's attention and you will be called into office where you will insist on leaving the club.

Level 4—Capabilities and Strategies: The behaviour you choose depends on your capabilities and strategies. For example, you may feel confident enough to approach the coach and ask what was behind the decision. On the other hand, you might be somewhat unsure and resort instead on telling your teammate the coach has got it wrong.

Level 3—Beliefs and Values: The capabilities and strategies you choose will depend on your beliefs and values. If you believe that you are an important part of team and a good performer who has a lot to offer when you get the opportunity to play, then you would more than likely go up to the coach and ask why you were left off. However, if you felt you or the coach were inadequate and you were left out because of your ability or coach's ability to understand the game (even without asking them), you may look for the exit strategy and tell your teammates what a ridiculous decision it was.

Level 2—Identity and Mission: Your beliefs and values are determined by your identity. If you see yourself as a good performer, then it is very possible that you would hold the belief that you are an important part of the team. If you were unable to play, you would be interested in finding a suitable replacement to you who will be able to perform.

Level 1—Spirituality and Purpose: Your identity is dependent on your purpose in your sport and the effect you wish to have on your team and your sport. Your purpose could be your contribution, helping your team to win, or simply enjoying yourself.

Depending on which of the six Logical Levels you choose, you can create a long-lasting, sustainable change in your sport and in your personal consistency. Making a change at a lower Logical Level (such as 6: Environment—you go to a different team) may or may not affect an upper level. Change at an upper level (such as 3: Belief) will affect all the levels below it.

Using Logical Levels to Explain and Understand Change

Using Logical Levels can lead to interesting explanations and discoveries.

Short-term vs. long-term consistency: Sometimes people find that attending a course, buying a book, or seeing a coach worked great at changing an aspect of their game for a short period of time, but eventually the unwanted behaviour returned. How can this be? It happens because if the new behaviour was made at a lower level and not in alignment with the person's beliefs, values, or identity, the higher level will override the lower level.

For change at the behaviour level to be long term and produce the ingredients of a successful career, the desired behaviour change must either be in alignment with a higher level or the change must take place at a high level; e.g., Level 2—Identity.

Making changes: Have you ever bought a new pair of boots? Purchased some new training gear? Started training with a different team? These are changes at the lowest Logical Level of Environment. Do you think it will be long-lasting? It will be only if the change is in alignment with the higher levels.

Have you ever started going to the gym to do extra sessions and get in tip-top shape (Level 5: Behaviours)? Have you ever learnt some new techniques in order to better participate in your sport (Level 4: Capability and Strategy). You may perform better for short period of time but then regress to how you performed before because you did not make a change at a higher Logical Level.

Sports and Career: Suppose you have a goal for yourself, but it is not in alignment with one of the higher levels. How successful do you think you will be in achieving your goal? For example, I know many people who like the idea of doing things, but actually doing it is not what they want. They like the idea of being a sports star because they think it will bring them fame and fortune, but they don't like the idea of working hard and training while every one else is out partying.

Albert Einstein once said, "The problems of today can only be solved at a higher level of thinking than that which created them." I have heard many people refer to this quote, but few can explain how to actually move to a higher level of thinking in order to accomplish it. Using Logical Levels, you can easily explain it. For example, if there is a problem at the Behavioural level, you must move to at least the Capability and Strategy level to solve it. NLP can assist you in making change at the higher levels or help you to ensure that your goals are aligned at all levels. Once this happens, your goals in life often become clear and are obtained effortlessly.

How to Make Sure All the Levels Are in Alignment

Building a Team Through Logical Levels

You can only observe the two lowest of the Logical Levels in another person—Behaviour and Environment. However, this will give you some idea as to their Capabilities and Strategies, Beliefs and Values, etc. To really be sure, you need to engage them in a conversation on these subjects. Having conversations with another person at the higher Logical Levels provides you with a more intimate understanding of that person and why they behave the way they do. How often do you have a conversation with someone you really care about and the topic is the weather (Environment) or what they are doing (Behaviour) rather than who they see themselves being (Identity and Mission) or what are they think (Beliefs and Values). To engage in this type of conversation, you need to create a space where each of you feels safe in disclosing your "inner selves."

A successful team, such as Manchester United, managed by Sir Alex Ferguson, has produced many victories over the years. All of the team has the desire to keep winning. Even after winning several matches and trophies, the winning does not stop. If any player does not conform, new players are brought in who buy into that winning culture.

Using Logical Levels to Identify Where Conflicts Exist With Your Players

How many people partake in a sport only to realise they are not suitable, it's not what they want to do, it's not for them? How many teams have deep divisions between management and players? How many of the conflicts on a team exist because of misalignment of the higher Logical Levels?

A number of years ago I was hired to observe a team and found that the desire, ambitions, and attitudes of some of the coaches and most of the players were completely different on many levels. This detrimentally effected the functionality of the team.

I used the Logical Levels to determine where the problems were originating. My findings were:

Level 1: Spirituality and Purpose (connection to a larger system): The players desired the connection while the coaches were disconnected.

Level 2: Identity and Mission (the reason for participating in a sport): Well-trained professional footballers can produce an exciting brand of football. Poorly trained professional footballers are often too discouraged to perform in any decent fashion.

Level 3: Beliefs and Values (the fitness skills and abilities to win matches): Many of the players thought it was important to play a style of football that enabled them to win matches and entertain the fans. They desired two training sessions per day, workouts in the gym, and coaching in techniques. The players had not gone into the sport to spend a high proportion of the time participating in non-productive training sessions and aiming just to survive in the league. Some of the coaches preferred to spend the afternoon at the golf course.

Level 4: Capabilities/Strategies (determining what is needed from everyone to win matches): The players wanted positive strategies for participating in a match, better planning of sessions, extra sessions, and more individualised training. From the coaches I saw less than supportive (and in some cases dysfunctional) capabilities and strategies as they would schedule short training sessions and take every afternoon off.

Level 5: Behaviours (how people react to their environment): The behaviours of competent, confident, motivated, and professional footballers when they are training in the right environment on well-kept training grounds is very different when the players are asked to perform at a less-than-suitable venue. The players exhibited distressed behaviours such as being fed up and feeling like walking out.

Level 6: Environment (the venue in which they must perform): Let's just say it was inadequate.

Using Logical Levels it was easy to see why the relationship between the players and coaches was a problem. A few of the coaches were excellent and always worked at the highest Logical Levels rather than going through the motions. The others were driven to put in as little as possible while still expecting to get out as much as possible. They neglected existing players, believing they weren't good enough for high aspirations. Somewhere along the way, the team had lost its key priority and focus on providing a match of which their fans could be proud.

Aligning Logical Levels for Personal Congruence

Could you use a similar approach with your team or your players that would allow them to see a situation differently and to draw on their strengths to overcome a perceived obstacle? For many of us, the Logical Levels operate outside of our conscious awareness, but whether we are aware of them or not, they have a significant influence over the quality of our lives.

The following exercise will help you to (1) become consciously aware of what factors influence how you live your life, (2) identify possible conflicts, and (3) recognize possible changes you can make to bring the levels more into alignment and hence achieve a higher level of personal congruence (reduced inner conflict). I suggest you take your time doing this exercise and write down your answers.

+ What is your Spirituality and Purpose? For the larger system (i.e., yourself, family, teammates, fans), what is your purpose or the impact you wish to have?

+ What is your Identity and Mission? Who are you or what role do you play in your sport? Are you a coach who helps performers fulfil their potential? Do you help the team win as a player? Do you bring fans enjoyment? Do you win for personal gratification or team gratification? Is your role the one necessary to achieve your purpose? What do you need to change?

+ What is your Beliefs and Values? What beliefs do you have about yourself and others in your sport in general? Do these beliefs support you in fulfilling your role? What do you value in yourself, in others, and in your sport in general? Are these values in alignment with your role? Are there other beliefs and values that you could take on that would be more in alignment?

+ What are your Capabilities and Strategies? What capabilities, strategies, or action plans do you have? Do you need to develop new capabilities, strategies or action plans? Are they in alignment with each of the Logical Levels? If not, what needs to be changed? Maybe you need to change your capabilities—get more training, improve your technique, get fitter, etc.—your strategies, or your action plans. Or maybe, given this new information, you need to reassess your purpose, your role or your beliefs and values.

+ What are your Behaviours? What do people really see or /experience in your behaviours? Are your behaviours in alignment with each of the Logical Levels? Does something need to be changed?

+ What is your Environment? When, where, and with whom do you demonstrate these behaviours? What is your relationship with your coach? Your teammates? Are your behaviours in alignment with all the Logical Levels?

Aligning Your Goals with Your Logical Levels

Many of the goals you have in your chosen sport may be based on the requests, desires or expectations of others—the coaches, your parents, spouse, teachers, and society. These are not your goals and hence do not have the energy that propels you forward to truly achieve your goals. When you struggle with your goals, almost always there is some hidden inner conflict that must be resolved. Often you are less then fully alive because of these inner conflicts. The previous questions will assist you in identifying these conflicts and realigning your goal with who you really are.

Think about your goals and answer the same questions for the Logical Levels as you did in the previous exercise. Notice if there is an alignment between the answers. For example you may find that achieving your goals would take time away from being with your spouse and children (assuming this is an important value for you). If this is the case, is there some way to adjust your goals or your Strategies and Action plan to spend time with your family and still achieve your goals? You may wish to ask those affected by your goals what they think as they often come up with solutions that you would never think of.

This process will allow you to become aware of the alignment (or lack of it) between your inner self and your goals. As you fine-tune your goals and align them with your inner self, you should find that your goals become clearer, more compelling, and more easily achieved. You will have a stronger sense of fulfilment and understanding of your role in your sport.

Chapter 4

Dare to Dream

"Regret can describe not only the dislike for an action that has been committed, but also regret of inaction. Many people find themselves wishing that they had done something in a past situation. Most people regret the things they haven't done, not the things they have."

—Anonymous

As a child, did you ever have a dream? What did you want to be and do? Did you ever imagine kicking the winning goal at Wembley Stadium in front of 80,000 cheering fans? Hitting the winning put at Augusta? Serving for a Wimbledon title? Winning the 100 metres sprint finals?

You may have mentioned your dream to one of your teachers, parents, family, and friends. Perhaps you were told you weren't good enough, clever enough, or talented enough.

What would you like to achieve as a coach or a performer? If you were approaching the end of the last match of your career, what would you be thinking? What are some of the dreams you once had but put away?

Life is short and you owe it to yourself to do the best possible and be what you want to be. Every dream starts with a vision. Did you ever have a vision or do you have a vision? Do you have a dream?

Take a few minutes to write down your dream.

LIVING A DREAM

All things are possible if you dare to dream. You have the most amazing, powerful resource at your disposal: your mind. We are all wired up with the same resources within that mind, but it's how you use those resources that make the difference.

Some people dream big and go for it. Some people decide to dream within the realms of what they perceive as reality. It never ceases to amaze me what is possible when people let their mind just wander and flow.

The following exercise was developed after talking with some of the greatest sporting minds in the world and eliciting the most amazing strategies and ideas. In order to use the same strategies with your mind, let your mind wander and know you don't have to tie yourself into anything you don't want to. Even if you don't follow up the thoughts, rest assured every one will reward you in some way.

I remember working with established premiership goal keeper Carlo Nash when he was playing for Crystal Palace football club. His story was unique as he had been released as an apprentice at a professional club and was playing non league. It wasn't until he was playing in the FA Vase cup final for a semi pro team that he was scouted by Crystal Palace football club. The rest is history. Carlo never gave up on his dream, but many young players who get released or suffer a set back, give up.

Exercise: Turning a Vision Into a Dream, a Dream Into Reality

Write down as many things as possible that you would like to achieve. Let your mind run wild. You are not accountable to any idea. Just have some fun.

- Think of a time when you were really creative or when you were making some very creative choices. It might have been a time when you were on a beach relaxing, going for a country walk, having a meal with family and friends, or listening to some music. Relive that time and remember what it felt like. What colours and images did you see? What could you hear? Close your eyes and let your mind run completely free, relax, and go into a creative state.

- Once you are in your creative state, think about your life's purpose. What are you here for? What are you passionate about? If you could do anything, what would it be? If money and time was no object what would you like to do? Imagine living in a world with no limitations, even for a few minutes; have some fun.

- Think of a time when you were realistic about some plan and put it into action in an effective way. It might have been your own plan or somebody else's. It could have been when you completed a course, set up a business, or went travelling, As you recall this time, relive the experience. Think about what you saw, what it felt like, what you heard.

- While you are in your realistic state of mind, come up with some logistics for implementing your new dream. What are some of the resources you would require if you were to implement it? How would you plan, allocate your time, or invest?

- Think of a time when you criticised a plan in a constructive way. When you saw weaknesses, as well as strengths, and identified problems and offered solutions. Again it might be your plan or someone else's. As you recall this time, relive the experience. Think of the images you saw, the feelings you felt, and what you heard.

- Gathering your thoughts in your critical mindset, come up with potential pitfalls of the dream, such as cost and time.

- Now, think once again of a time when you were really creative. Relive that time. What did it feel like, what did you see, what could you hear? Let your mind run free, relax and go into its creative state. As you let your mind wander, notice what you learnt from the time you relived in steps 3 and 4. How does this affect your ideas and plans for the way you would like to live?

Implementing Your Dream

What dream or dreams do you have that have sprung to mind and you're a ready to take out of your cupboard? Be excited, get excited, be passionate about it, knowing you have awakened your mind again. Remember, it's never too late to implement your dreams and there is no better time than the present. A dream is only fantasy unless you take action.

Chapter 5

Setting Goals and Staying Motivated

"Keep away from people who try to belittle your ambitions. Small people always do that, but the really great make you feel that you, too, can become great."

—Mark Twain

Whether you realise it or not, goals are a fundamental part of achieving excellence at sports. The two choices you have are either to carry on leaving things to chance in your event or sport ,or you take control of your participation and perform in a way that brings you fulfilment, purpose and achievement.

When you set goals, you may experience the fear of not achieving them. What if you set awesome goals only to fall flat on your face and not achieve them, what then? Well, I think the most amazing thing about setting goals is the journey and although sometimes we don't achieve what we set out to achieve, we achieve something more significant. More often than not, in the process of working towards and achieving goals, many other possibilities open up and we achieve so much more than we set out to do.

After your have listed your goals, I will then show you a powerful technique for achieving your goals.

YOUR GOAL-SETTING STRATEGY

Create a Vision Board

Get a piece of poster board and attach it to a wall in your dressing room, locker or home where you will see it often. As you go through magazines, brochures, etc., and you see pictures of the things you want—such as a picture of grounds and the stadiums you would like to compete at and the performers you would love to challenge—cut them out and glue them to your vision board. In other words, make yourself a collage of the goals that excite you knowing that when you look at them every day, they will soon be yours.

Determine Your Goals

Write one goal you have for each of the following categories. You may think of others, but for now write one goal for each category.

- **Technically:** improve your golf swing, tennis serve, free kicking in football, goal kicking in rugby, etc.
- **Characteristics:** Is any part of your mindset holding you back—self belief, self esteem, confidence? Is there any part of the way that you behave that upsets you? If so, set a goal to improve your behaviour or find a solution to the problem.
- **Career:** What are your aspirations? At what level do you want to play? Who do you want to compete against? What level of your sport do you wish to reach—amateur, semi pro, professional?
- **Education:** What would you like to learn? About your sport? About your role?
- **Tactically:** How would you like to improve tactically?
- **Physically:** What are your physical goals? What is your level of fitness (determined through fitness testing)? What is your speed? Your power? Your stamina? Your agility?
- **Process:** How many goals are you aiming to score in your season? What is the distance you want to hit a golf ball? How fast do you want to run a certain distance?
- **Spiritual and Contribution:** What is the biggest contribution you want to make in your sport (your intrinsic-values and enjoyment)? Do you want to entertain fans? Do you want to receive enjoyment from playing the sport?

Now, choose one of the goals from the above category. A common question many people ask is if they can set more than one goal. Of course you can, you can set as many goals as you wish to ensure growth, particularly for different aspects of your sport. However, I would suggest using the strategy and the following exercise for only one goal until you develop your action plan. After that you can set different action plan for different goals.

Goal Setting

Using the following powerful strategy you can take your one goal and put into action.

State the Goal

Stating your goal, positively and specifically, is your road map to achieving it, especially if you are just starting out in a new sport, playing a certain level, or experiencing a certain level of ability.

- What do you want to achieve, what would you like to happen, what outcome do you want?
  - State your goal in positive terms. The mind cannot process a negative instruction; for example, if I say, "Don't think about the colour red," what comes to mind?
  - Make your goal so specific a 5-year-old can understand it. For example, if you want to play professionally, stating your goal that way is vague and not specific enough. Instead, write down the ideal team you want to play for or the exact level or league in which you want to play. State the type of team you want to play on. Declare what tournaments you would like to win. Be as specific as possible.
  - Where do you want to be once you have achieved your goal? For example, do you want to be a professional athlete competing in the European circuit? Do you want to run the 100 metres in under 10 seconds? Do you want to play semi-pro football for a certain team scoring 20 goals per season? Do you want to complete a marathon in less than 3 hours?

Specify the Goal in Sensory-Based Terms

We learn through our senses and build pathways in our mind through our senses which makes reality...well...real. Engage all of your senses in this description process to employ more of your brain and nervous system.

- Close your eyes and imagine what it would be like to have achieved your goal. What will you see? Hear? Feel?
- Determine what steps or stages are involved in reaching this goal and what it will feel like as you complete each step.
- Formulate a plan to determine what steps are necessary in achieving the goal. Feel yourself completing each one. For example, step 1 might be to email or phone someone, step 2 might be to get in peak fitness (feel the muscle burn that comes from working out), step 3 might be to improve technique (visualise yourself working at a technique until you perfect it), and step 4 might be to set up a trial.

Specify the Goal in a Way You Find Compelling

In order for a goal to have meaning, you need to specify your goal in a meaningful way. Imagine the steps you have undergone to reach your goal. See yourself achieving your goal as though you are watching yourself on TV. Notice the clarity of the image. See what you are wearing and what the people around you are wearing. See the surroundings. Hear what you are saying, what the people around you are saying. Feel the emotions you think you would feel seeing yourself achieve the goal.

+ What would achieving the goal mean to you? To your family?
+ What effect will achieving this goal have on the greater community?
+ Is the goal compelling? Does it make you excited?

Run an Ecological Check on Your Goal

There are always consequences when you work towards or achieve your goals. Are you willing to make the necessary sacrifices? Accept how it could affect your life? Make sure your goal is good for you in all areas of your life. Make sure it's what you want for you.

+ Is the desired goal right for you in all circumstances of your life?
+ Is your goal appropriate in all your personal relationships?
+ What will having your goal give you that you do not now have?
+ What implications does it have on other parts of your life (e.g., spending time with your children, your partner, your family)?
+ Is your goal achievable?

The Plan

Visualise the where, when, how, with whom, etc., you will need in order to reach this goal.

+ Where? For example, celebrating winning a trophy, making a team at a certain level, or running New York Marathon.
+ When? Set a time limit. Set the date, and even the time, for when you will achieve your goal. For example, I will be playing professional football by 12/10 /2012. I will be scoring x amount of goals by 2014. I will win the league by 2016.
+ How? State step-by-step how you intend to achieve your goal. Generate a plan to do so. For example, get into peak fitness, improve my technique, hire a personal trainer, an agent, a promoter, phone up for trials.
+ Whom? List of the resources that can help you achieve your goal. For example, people, family, friends, teammates, coaches, colleagues, etc.

State the Resources Needed to Achieve the Goal

+ What resources will you need in order to achieve this goal?
+ Who will you have to become?

- Who else has achieved this goal?
- Have you ever had or done this before?
- Do you know anyone who has?
- What prevents you from moving towards it and attaining it now?

Evidence the Procedure

- How will you know when your goal has been realized? How many times have you achieved a goal without even realising it? It's important to know when you have realised your goal. You wouldn't climb Mount Everest and not take a moment to admire the view.
- What will let you know that you have attained your desired state? How many people achieve a goal and think, "Is that it?" You need to identify the feelings that will come with achieving your goal. Close your eyes and think about what feelings you will have once you have achieved your goal.

Place Your Goal on a Timeline

- Placing your goal on a timeline gives you the opportunity to note the progress you are making, step by step, in reaching that goal.

Once you have completed these steps, you will be able to write down the essentials of your goal, starting with the end in mind. At the very top of the page, write specifically what your goal is and the exact date you will achieve it. For example:

- **July 2012:** run 100 metres in 10 seconds; play for certain team in top league; play certain golf handicap.
- **March 2012:** run 100 metres in 10.4 seconds; play for a team in the second highest league.
- **January 2012:** run 100 metres 10.6 seconds; play for a team in the third highest league.
- **December 2011:** run 100 metres in 10.8 seconds; play for a team in the fourth highest league.
- **August 2011:** enter competitions for 100 metres sprints; set up trial with pro sports team.
- **June 2011:** hire athletic coach, begin intensive fitness training for football, improve technique, join athletic team, set up meeting with agent with an eye to play pro football.

Making Your Goals Manageable

These steps bring a sense of reality to achieving your goals and makes them manageable. After the exercise you will find a chart that you can use to break down your goals into a time frame.

- **Step 1:** Write down what you envision for yourself in 10-years time. Write down your goals in list form using complete sentences. Use adjectives and be specific. Instead of writing "playing professional football," write "I am playing for a successful professional team, winning trophies, and bringing enjoyment to the lives of others."
- **Step 2:** Create tasks for each goal—task 1, 2, 3, etc. Assign each task a due date; e.g., today, tomorrow, next year, etc. Begin each task with an action verb. Instead of writing "sprint coaching," write "Enrol in golf, tennis, football team, etc.
- **Step 3:** Write down what you envision for yourself in one year as a milestone to know you are on track. Use your list of 10-year goals as a template.
- **Step 4:** Create tasks for each one-year goal. Use your list of tasks for your 10-year goals as a template. Assign each goal at least one task per week.
- **Step 5:** Place your lists in a visible location, such as on your bedroom wall or somewhere else that you look at daily.
- **Step 6:** Write your goals and tasks on a calendar. Put the tasks on their corresponding due dates. Write the goals onto estimated dates or dates of completion.
- **Step 7:** Use the lists and calendar as a template for one-week tasks, one-month goals, 10-year goals, and other time frames.

Use the following chart to outline the time required to achieve your goals. Write down where you want to be in relation to achieving your goal at each time frame. In this chart you will write your long-term, medium-term, and short-term goals and include the miles stones along the way.

Long-Term Goals

10 years: _____

_____

5 years: _____

_____

3 years: _____

_____

2 years: _____

_____

1 year: _____

_____

3 months _____

_____

1 month _____

_____

Weekly Goals

Action Plans are essential if you're going to get the most out of your time. Weekly planning helps you to decide how to make effective use of your time. Write down the daily tasks that will take you closer to achieving your goals. Work proactively rather than reactively.

Time	Mon	Tues	Wed	Thurs	Fri	Sat	Sun
6am–7am	task 1,2,3 (i.e. phone coach, email, go for run to build aerobic fitness)						
7am–8am							
8am–9am							
9am–10am							
10am–11am							
11am–12pm							
12pm–1pm							
1pm–2pm							
2pm–3pm							
3pm–4pm							
4pm–5pm							
5pm to 6pm							
6pm–7pm							
7pm–8pm							

Chapter 6

Self Talk

*"They may forget what you said, but they will
never forget how you made them feel."*

—Carl W. Buechner

Words have power. Think of some of the most inspirational speeches you have heard. A word can affect people because for them the association to that word may have a much deeper implication or meaning. The same can be said about words spoken in a positive way—a thank you, please, well done—can go a long way.

Have you ever sat in the dressing room before the start of a match and the coach gave a speech or found the right words to inspire you and the team? Have you done something well during a match and nobody acknowledged you or gave you any praise? Do you remember the differences in the way you felt?

Seligman analyzed the explanatory styles of sports teams and found that the more optimistic teams created more positive synergy and performed better than the pessimistic ones.

Of all the people you with whom you interact on a daily basis, the most important person you will ever communicate with is yourself.

At this point you're probably thinking, "Communicate with myself?" Yes, you do communicate with yourself and the effect your inner dialogue has on our life is immense. Often you are our own worst critic.

We all carry on an inner dialogue that can have a big influence on how we think and feel. It has been established by psychologists and neuroscientists that we maintain an ongoing dialog, or self-talk, of between 150 and 300 words a minute. This works out to a dialog of between 45,000 and 51,000 words a day. Most of our self-talk is harmless dialog that revolves around our daily activities like, "I need to stop at the shop to pick up some milk…I wonder what's on television tonight…What should we have for dinner?"

The danger of this inner dialogue in the context of sports is when it takes on a negative undertone related to our participation as a coach or athlete, such as, "I am not good enough to play at this level…I am useless. I always mess things up…I can't handle the pressure, we always lose at penalties…I haven't got the natural ability to play sports." The ongoing negative reinforcement created by habitual negative self-talk

Choose your words carefully. What you say to yourself or your team can directly affect performance.

results in the creation of a limiting belief(s) that goes on to become a self-fulfilling prophecy. Your parents, family, partners, teachers, coaches, teammates, fans, and friends have such an effect on you that their words can become buried in your brain and phrases echo around your head. Sometimes you hear your parent's comments in a situation you've experienced before, only this time you're telling yourself the same thing! If you hear the same negative comments too often, you may begin to believe they are true. Take a moment to think about your inner self dialogue, and the effect it is having on your life. Think of some of words going through your mind.

It is estimated by research that it's necessary for the ratio of positive comments to negative comments to be at least five to one for a relationship to be healthy and survive long term. For these reasons, it is important not to let others put you down. Even more important is not to put yourself down.

Your self talk can shape your ability to perform in sports and influence your attitude and behaviour towards your participation and how you respond to certain situations in a match, such as whether you have the confidence to express yourself during a game or to attempt a new technique or skill. It can increase your stress levels, limit your potential, and influence your outlook on an experience.

LANGUAGE IS INFLUENTIAL

Inevitably, every coach will hunger for the right words when trying to communicate with his team, whether the situation is before a big game, after a loss, or while overcoming adversity. Articulating the right idea in words can be important in the ongoing drive for success. There is always a need for saying the right thing at the right time.

If you've been told by a teammate that someone in your team is completely useless, you will probably perceive that person as more incapable than if you had been told, "They need assistance with certain tasks" or "They need a bit of guidance."

Limited by Your Vocabulary

If you say, "I will never be good at this...I don't deserve it...I am stupid...I can't do this...This is not for me...I don't deserve it," it is more likely that you will experience defeat or disappointment. This is because your subconscious mind tends to believe the thoughts it hears. You can limit your abilities by telling yourself "I can't... this is too hard...I shouldn't even try."

I worked with a group of football coaches that would stand on the touchline and shout to the players at the top of their voices, "Don't lose the ball. Don't foul. Don't miss the target." Inevitably, that would be exactly what would happen on the field. The negativity would rub off on the players and they would lose the ball, foul, and miss the target.

I conversed with one of the players and he said he felt stifled and afraid to make a mistake. I asked him to tell me a list of phrases and words going through his head whilst playing and they were all negative. We transformed his inner dialogue from feeling stifled to feeling powerful. The use of language had a massive impact in getting him back into form.

Exercise

Take a few moments to write down some of the things you say to yourself. As you write, imagine the effect these words are having on your life. For example:

+ How would you describe your ability to participate in your sport?
+ How would you describe yourself as a sports person or coach?

One of my clients had a list of over 50 negative statements he was saying to himself over and over again in his mind. Whilst driving to training, he found himself saying, "I hate this team, but I am too useless to find a better team." Every time he made a mistake he would call himself a moron, a useless idiot, good for nothing. Even when

> Watch your thoughts; they become words. Watch your words; they become actions.
> Watch your actions; they become habits. Watch your habits; they become character.
> Watch your character; it becomes your destiny.
>
> —Author Unknown

he was playing a match, he would find himself saying, "This team is out of my league. I am not good enough to play against a team like this." And the list went on.

I asked my client, "How important is it for you to succeed as a footballer?"

"It's all I ever wanted to do," he replied.

"When did you first have the dream of being a footballer?" I inquired.

He said he had wanted to play football from 4 years of age. I asked him that if he was coaching a 4-year-old who had a dream of being a footballer, would he call the child a moron, a useless idiot, a good for nothing? Appalled, he said he wouldn't.

Some of the things we find acceptable to say to ourselves, we wouldn't dream of saying to anyone else because we know the effect it would have on our relationship with the person. Well the most important relationship you will ever have is with yourself. Make positive comments to yourself.

Here are some techniques you can implement to transform your inner dialogue:

+ **Thought-Stopping:** As you notice yourself saying something negative in your mind, you can stop your thought mid-stream by saying to yourself "Stop!" Saying this aloud will be even more powerful. Having to say it aloud will make you more aware of how many times and where throughout the day you are stopping negative thoughts.

+ **Rubber-Band Snap:** Another therapeutic trick is to walk around with a rubber band around your wrist. When you notice negative self-talk, pull the band away from your skin and let it snap back. It will hurt a little and serve as a slightly negative consequence that will make you both more aware of your thoughts and help to stop them! If you don't want to subject yourself to walking around with a rubber band on your wrist, be even more careful to limit the negative thoughts!

Turn a Negative into a Positive

+ Describe a situation in your sport when you tend to think or talk negatively to yourself.

+ Identify the negative statement you say to yourself.

+ Identify words or thoughts you can use to help you stop the negative thoughts.
+ List positive, beneficial statements you can use to replace your negative thoughts. These should be meaningful to you.

Positive Language

The main reason for giving a positive instruction is the mind does not understand how to process a negative instruction. For example, if I say to you, "Don't think of a purple elephant," what do you think of? The very thing I told you not to do!

By using positive instructions, stating what you want rather than what you don't want, can have a powerful positive effect on the mind. Using negative instructions produces negative thoughts. For example, if a football coach says to his players, "Don't lose the ball" or "When you shoot, don't miss the target," losing the ball and missing the target will be all they think about. It would be better to instruct the player to hit the target, to keep possession. Phrases such as "don't foul…don't lose the ball…don't lose the game," can all be replaced by more positive instructions.

Positive Self Talk

List five negative comments you say to yourself (such as, "I am hopeless. I will never be good at this") and replace them with positive comments. For example, if you make an error in your game, don't call yourself an idiot and tell yourself you always make that mistake. Instead, ask yourself what you can learn from the mistake and use that knowledge to improve the situation. Focus on the outcome you want.

1. _____
2. _____
3. _____
4. _____
5. _____

Write down positive comments that can replace them (such as "I am an amazing person. I have learnt many techniques in the past and will learn more in the future")?

1. _____
2. _____
3. _____
4. _____
5. _____

Giving Instructions

List five negative instructions you give to your players, performers, or teammates and replace them with five positive instructions. For example, a coach may tell his players, "Don't lose the ball." A more favourable instruction would be, "Keep possession." Focus on the outcome you want!

Negative Instructions

1. _____
2. _____
3. _____
4. _____
5. _____

Positive Instructions

1. _____
2. _____
3. _____
4. _____
5. _____

You can transform the way you perform in your sport by using the power of words. The more you work at this, the easier it becomes. The impact of changing even one negative word to something more positive can completely change your mindset and outlook on your sport.

Chapter 7

Metaphorically Speaking

"Float like a butterfly, sting like a bee"

—Muhammad Ali

Do you remember some of the stories you heard when you were young, stories such as Cinderella or the Ugly Duckling? You were able to draw metaphors from these stories to get a sense of perspective of your life and deal with problems such as the first time you had your heart broken or were rejected by the school cheerleading squad or football team. Throughout your life, these stories and metaphors galvanised your resolve when meeting life's challenges.

THE POWER OF A METAPHOR

"Metaphor" is based on a Greek word meaning "to carry something across or transfer." Metaphors provide you with hope and light and help you to draw on inner resources to find meaning in difficult and challenging situations. Metaphors provide you with multiple perspectives. They give you the ability to step out of the problem and see it from a different perspective, to shift your mindset to a more creative solution. Metaphors can have a positive or negative effect on your sport because they can completely alter your perceptions and make an impact on how you feel and play your sport.

A powerful, negative example would be "Same shit, different day." I remember seeing the phrase on bumper stickers and even printed on tee shirts. Imagine waking up with that perspective on life! Imagine what state of mind these people had. Probably not the best. I am sure we all have come across, and have possibly used, many other negative metaphors for work, relationships, and sports.

How about these?

"My game is like a roller coaster…They couldn't organise a piss up in a brewery… He couldn't hit a barn door (metaphor used for someone who is struggling to score goals)."

A metaphor can change your whole perception of a situation. It can move you out of a problematic situation, put you in a more resourceful state of mind, make you happier, or give you hope.

Have you ever watched the film Forrest Gump? Forrest tells us, "My momma always said, 'Life is like a box of chocolates. You never know what you're going to get.'"

Throughout the film, Forrest's attitude and outlook on life is one of anticipation. He takes all of life's events in his stride. A positive metaphor such as Forrest's can be very influential in the way you live your life and in forming your behaviour and outlook on your sport and your life.

> When you walk through a storm
> Hold your head up high
> And don't be afraid of the dark
> At the end of the storm
> There's a golden sky
> And the sweet silver song of a lark

When I was working with the Bury football club, a player named Colin Kazim Richards came through. He had come up from the depths of League 2 and would go on to champion's league football and achieve amazing success. I set a physical training programme for the players and had them run tough, 400 meter sprints. Colin didn't particularly enjoy this part of training. When he let me know his thoughts about doing the 400s, I said to him, "You're a machine. You're built like a machine." This metaphor transformed the way he perceived the training. I later bumped into Colin at a match and one of the things he said was, "I am a machine." It brought a smile to my face.

The following exercise is very powerful and can help you transform the way you feel about your life.

Exercise

Write down the metaphors you are using to run your mind. Think about the perceptions you gain from these metaphors. If the effect is negative, change it to something positive. Notice how different you feel by creating a more positive metaphor. For example:

+ Change "We are all just a drop in the ocean," to something like, "by throwing a pebble into a river, we can create a ripple."
+ Change "At work I am just a number," to something like, "I am an important cog in a wheel."
+ Change, "I am stuck in a dead-end team," to something like, "This is a stepping stone to better things."

Complete the following statements in a positive manner:

+ My team: _____

_____

+ My ability: _____

_____

+ My character: _____

_____

Using Metaphors to Create Stories

There is nothing better than a good sports story to inspire other athletes to develop an inner resolve and propel them to greatness or help them draw strength from someone else's adversity. It can change participation in a sport from the same old, same old to a bed of roses.

Some of the clients I work with have been through the most challenging experiences in sports and life—they have suffered physical injuries, loss of form and confidence, debilitating personal problems, and have gotten stuck in a negative place unable to move forward and make the most of their life. I ask these clients to come up with a metaphor for the situation they are going through; it often has a powerful effect on their life.

I was once working with a sports person who had a loss of form for several months. He felt negative and anxious. He told me he had no hope, no motivation, and found it difficult to participate in a sport he had once really enjoyed. He was going to give up playing his sport and cut himself off.

I asked him to write down a metaphor for the situation he was in but to close the metaphor with a positive ending. I told him to remove himself from his present state of mind and focus instead on his desired state of mind. Once it had been written down in this form, I told him to put it in a place where he could see it daily.

He completely transformed his game. He found top form again, started training extra sessions, joined a new team, and revitalized his career.

A Metaphor Example

Think of a river. Visualise that on its journey to the sea it meets many challenges and obstacles. No matter what gets in its way—hills, forests, fields, or dams—it manages to find a way around or through them. Regardless of how difficult, challenging, or impossible it may seem, the river keeps flowing until it meets the sea.

Create Your Own Metaphor

Using the above metaphor as an example, create a metaphor for a challenge you may be going through at the moment in your sport or your life. While writing your metaphor:

- Populate the metaphor with characters (superheroes, wizards, trees, birds, animals, people, etc.) and decide on the relationships of the people involved.
- Develop a plot that reflects the current problem. Include anything you may have already tried in order to change things.

- Develop the story so its moves towards a positive ending. Be creative and draw from your subconscious mind.
- Having created your metaphor, notice how differently you feel about the situation and how your perspective has changed.

Chapter 8

Believe in Yourself

"It's not who you are that holds you back, it's who you think you're not."
—Anonymous

In the first half of the 20th century, the world believed that it was impossible to run a mile under four minutes. When, on May 6, 1954, Roger Bannister ran a mile in 3.59 minutes, everyone was in awe. Then, a curious development took place. Within the following year, many other runners ran the mile under four minutes. It was as if a spell had been broken. To understand this phenomenon better, we have to take a closer look at our beliefs, and how they affect us.

Beliefs guide our decisions and behaviour in all areas of life, including sports. They determine what we think is or is not possible. More often than not they prove to be self-fulfilling prophecies. Most of our beliefs are not fully our own. There is every chance they have been modelled from other people.

Once a belief is formed, we work overtime to prove it right, even if the belief is something negative like, "I am never going to be good at this," or "I never get anything right." Many people are governed by their beliefs, even if they are harmful to others and themselves.

Some of the negative beliefs I have come across over the years when working with many sports people are (1) they will never achieve their aims, (2) they don't have the ability, (3) they won't become good, (4) they can't play at a certain level, and (5) they can't get motivated or lack confidence. The list goes on. To experience success as a coach or performer, it is essential to have a certain qualities. One the most important qualities is belief. If you believe you can achieve an outcome, your mind starts to recognise your positive qualities.

RECOGNISING YOUR BELIEFS

What is something you believed at some point that you thought you could not do in your sport or that it would be very difficult to do, even though you managed to do it? For example, playing at a certain level might have seemed a world away, hitting a golf ball a certain distance might have seemed impossible, or completing a 10-k run in under a certain time was beyond your ability.

Write down a belief that you may have had about yourself that changed.

> Many limiting beliefs are characterised by terms such as:
>
> Can't. Need, Have to, Must. Mustn't, Should or shouldn't

Then, write down positive beliefs you have at this moment about your ability in sports. For example: beliefs that you are fast, excellent technical ability, intelligent, etc.

Finally, write down negative beliefs you may have in your life that you may or may not know where you picked up. For example: beliefs that you will never play at a certain level, find a good team, develop a certain technical skill, or win a match.

Technique to Overcome Negative Beliefs

First, DO NOT challenge such limiting beliefs with a question "why" or "why not?" Let's look at some examples:

+ "I can't beat that opponent."
+ "I can't play at that level."
+ "I must be confident."
+ "I shouldn't get nervous."
+ "I should train harder."

By asking the question, "Why not?" you are likely to elicit a list of reasons which only justify and re-enforce the limiting belief rather than shifting it.

Instead, ask what. The "What" question focuses the brain in another direction. It helps you to look for practical suggestions and solutions within your control. For example:

+ "What would have to be different for me to play at that level?"
+ "What would have to be different for me to be confident?"
+ "What would have to be different for me to train harder?"

Creating Leverage and Releasing Negative Beliefs

Think of a negative belief you have about yourself and the sport you participate in, or a belief you wrote in the list earlier, that isn't serving you.

Write down a negative belief you have but that you want to release.

Now, having written the belief down, ask the following questions about the belief:

+ How is this belief ridiculous or absurd?
+ Was the person from whom I learnt this belief worth modelling in this area?

41

- What will it ultimately cost me if I don't let go of this belief?
- What will it cost me emotionally if I don't let go of this belief?
- What will is cost me in my relationships I don't let go of this belief?
- What will is cost me physically if I don't let go of this belief?
- What will it cost me financially if I don't let go of this belief?
- What will it cost my family and loved ones if I don't let go of this belief?

Having asked those questions, how do you feel about that negative belief? Is it worth keeping? If not let it go!

You don't have to believe anything about yourself you don't want to. You have a choice.

If you are still haven't found the leverage to break through the negative belief, it might mean there is some work to be done in a certain area. You didn't learn the skills to play your game overnight. It took years of training. You trained, watched other people play, and learnt from their example. A negative belief is also learnt over time. Try to figure out the source of the negative belief.

A useful exercise I use with my clients for releasing negative beliefs and prior to setting goals is a Belief Assessment Sheet. This helps identify where you are in relation to working towards a goal. Take any outcome you are unsure of and complete the following exercise. It will assist you in building the capabilities or provide you with more leverage to go for your outcome.

Exercise: Belief Assessment Sheet

Rate your beliefs on a scale of one to ten with ten being highest:

Do you believe your goal is achievable?

1 2 3 4 5 6 7 8 9 10

Do you believe you deserve your goal?

1 2 3 4 5 6 7 8 9 10

Do you believe your goal is appropriate and worthwhile?

1 2 3 4 5 6 7 8 9 10

Is your goal is desirable?

1 2 3 4 5 6 7 8 9 10

Do you know what you have to do to achieve your goal?

1 2 3 4 5 6 7 8 9 10

Do you have the skills and capabilities to achieve your goal?

1 2 3 4 5 6 7 8 9 10

Certain beliefs can serve you. There is good reason for assessing your capabilities to achieve certain tasks. For example, I was working with a client several years ago who wanted to run a marathon, though he had never done any running before. Whilst he believed it was within his capabilities to run the marathon, he also felt he needed to start with training and give himself a time frame to accomplish this goal with which he was comfortable.

Goal Setting

Set some goals to help you stay the course. Identify any areas in which you feel you need to develop and take action. With a sense of self-belief and certainty, you will achieve your outcome in time, just as you achieved other outcomes in your life. By using the same principles in chapter 5, complete the following goal-setting process to get you well on the way to developing aspects of your game.

1. **State your goal in the positive.**

   Think about what you want rather than what you don't want. If you still come up with something negative, ask yourself, "What do I want instead?" For example, at what level do I want to play in my sport? or "How fast do you want to run the 100 metres?"

2. **State it in simple terms.**

   If a five-year-old wouldn't understand the goal, it may be too complex. Unlike some other goal-setting techniques, your goal needs to be brief, simple and specific. For example, state exactly with which team or at what level you want to play, how many goals you want to score in the season, or how far you want to hit golf ball.

3. **State it in the present tense.**

   State it as if it is happening now. I have, I am, I'm doing…what you are doing right now.

4. **Is your goal achievable and realistic?**

   Has someone else already achieved this or might they achieve this? Is it realistic for you? If one person can achieve something, then so can you.

5. **Set a time and make it an exciting outcome.**

   There is some debate about setting a date and some people feel uncomfortable about this. If it is a small goal, then do it. If it is a really big goal, then I advise that you leave the time off for the moment until it starts to look like things are moving.

6. **How will you achieve your goal?**

    For example: I will achieve my goal by doing two extra training sessions a week, using weights to develop strength, practise my technique three times per week, incorporate visualisation strategy, etc. Do things in a manageable way to suit your lifestyle. Choose exercises and activities you enjoy and that are going to move you towards your goal. Remember not to overestimate what you can achieve in a week or underestimate what can be achieved in six months.

Chapter 9

See Things From a Different Point of View

"Do not judge a person until you walk two moons in his moccasins."
—Cheyenne Proverb

ave you ever had a disagreement with a coach or a teammate—been upset, angry, and disappointed about what was said—only to see the situation in a completely different light at another time in your life? Have you ever been hurt by what someone said or did? Have you felt let down and carried the emotion for a long period of time? Have you ever been a victim of someone's actions and found it difficult to move forward? Have you ever wanted a member of your team to perform in a certain way and been disappointed?

Sometimes we see things in a blinkered way, never considering another person's thoughts and feelings. It is easy to pass judgement on how someone else may handle a situation. What is more of a challenge, and may provide you with valuable insights, is seeing a situation from another point of view.

PERCEPTUAL POSITIONS

The Perceptual Positions techniques are taken from Neuro Linguistic Programming (NLP). Their goal is to show you, in a structured way, how to see another person's point of view. They are straightforward and can be done in just a few minutes.

The techniques in this chapter are very powerful when used in your personal life to resolve conflict, in business to alter your perceptions, and in sports to gain a stronger understanding of colleagues, opposition, critics, and fans. Seeing things from a different perception can help you move in a positive direction.

Examples of the Use of Perceptual Positions

I once used the Perceptual Positions exercises from this chapter with two teammates that hadn't spoken for nearly a whole season. After doing the exercise, they picked up the phone, decided to meet, and sort out their differences. Soon after that they played their best football of the season.

I recall when the then-manager of the Bury football club, Chris Casper, would always point out to the players how the opposition perceived certain situations in the context of a match. This would give the players a boost, knowing that whatever was going through their minds, the perception of them was one in which the opposition knew they were in for a tough game.

I once worked with an athlete who had been depressed for many years. When he was growing up, his parents had been very abusive, both physically and mentally. He said he felt low and wasn't sure if he could move forward with his sport.

It was hard for him to put the abuse behind him and focus, so we used the Perceptual Positions exercise to look at things from the perspective of his parents. After doing so, he finally felt free and alive and was able to pursue his dreams.

He felt his parents had only done what they knew how to do at a difficult time in their lives. They didn't know any better. He let go of the resentment and pain and decided that he was no longer going let what happened in his past dictate his future. He realized the pain and anger he felt was affecting only one person—him. Amongst many other positive changes, my client took his sport to a new level, training harder and more often.

No one has the right to continue to affect you through actions long past. You can claim back your life.

Perceptual Positions Technique for Sports Coaches

Step 1: The History

As you experience a situation with a particular player whilst coaching, you begin to remember other times when things did not go quite as well as you would have liked them to. As you mull this over in your mind, you start remembering the interaction (history) in greater detail.

Step 2: Seeing It Through Your Own Eyes

You see the experience through your own eyes, seeing the interaction between yourself and the player. You hear the experience through your own ears, listening to what the player said, hearing what you said, hearing the same thoughts you thought to yourself. You experience what it is like to coach this player, what you felt towards him and the trouble he gave you. Now, freeze the interaction and notice what you have learnt about yourself. During the freeze action you can perceive better ways of dealing with the situation, such as controlling (or hiding) your emotions, setting up better positioning, being stronger or more polite, and making your instructions clearer for the listener, etc.

Step 3: Through the Player's Eyes

See the experience through the player's eyes, becoming aware of what you look like from his perspective. You hear the experience through the player's ears, listening

There are usually two sides to any story. For example, you are disappointed with your children because you asked them to tidy their room and they haven't done so. You become angry and begin to think they are lazy and disrespectful. But, the reason your children didn't tidy their room is because they stayed up late the last two nights trying to finish an assignment they were finding difficult. They tried to talk to you about it but you didn't come home from work until just before they went to bed. You were tired and as soon as you got home you switched on the television and slumped on the sofa. Because of this, both you and your children are angry and hurt and are blaming each other for the problem.

to what you are saying. You feel what it is like to be the player, what he might feel about you. Now, freeze the interaction and notice what you have learnt about the player. It is during this freeze action that you can imagine what the player thought about you as you were dealing with him. Would the situation have worked better if you had been calmer? If you had used different words? Perhaps you could have been more authoritative, more friendly, more polite. Did you really need to embarrass him? Next time this incident happens, you should now be able to temper your approach to eliminate the things that did not originally work.

Step 4: Through the Eyes of an Observer

See the experience through the eyes of a neutral observer. You listen to the coach and the player talking to one another. You become aware of how they have interacted previously in the game and notice patterns and repetitions. Then you freeze the interaction and perceive what you have learnt about the coach and the player. Was there a clash of two strong characters? Who was in charge of the situation? Was the situation resolved in a satisfactory way? How was the situation managed?

Step 5: Using the New Perceptions to Improve

What have you learnt? What could you do to resolve any issues? Have you improved your ability to handle different situations which may arise?

One of life's challenges is to have the strength to see things from a different point of view. It isn't easy because it might highlight your flaws. It's easier to believe you are always right or that you have been unfairly hurt or upset and feel victimized by someone's actions. You may feel that seeing a situation from someone else's point of view is irrelevant.

The art of seeing things from a different point of view is an opportunity for you to take action, release any negative emotions, take a level of responsibility to move things forward, and effect things in a positive way.

Chapter 10

Getting in the Zone

"Concentration is the ability to think about absolutely nothing when it is absolutely necessary."

—Ray Knight

Competition can bring out the best or the worst in athletes. The psychological demands are especially high when two individuals or teams are striving to achieve the same goals. When physical skills are evenly matched, it is often the competitor who can control his or her mind before and during the sporting event, who wins. However, many athletes wrongly assume that the mental aspects of performance are innate and unchangeable when, in reality, systematic mental training can have a similar impact on performance as physical workouts.

The mental aspects prior to any performance should involve focusing on what you are going to do during the event. Whether it is participating in top flight sports, delivering a sales presentation, teaching a lesson to group of students, going for job interview, or meeting someone new, being in right frame of mind at the right time is crucial.

Many athletes have routines to get into the right state of mind. Golfers may follow a routine that allows them to prepare in the same way for each shot, as do tennis players before serving or rugby place kickers before kicking (remember the image of Jonny Wilkinson, the famous English rugby kicker, clenching his hands while preparing to take a kick for a goal). Is it a pre-performance routine or superstition when Nomar Garciaparra refastens his batting gloves between every pitch? What about when Dirk Nowitzki sings David Hasselhoff tunes before he shoots free throws. The key to any routine is that it provides the athlete with control and directs attention to the important cues. Coaches and athletes should work together in deciding the key attention cues and the sequence in which these should occur.

There are many potential distractions for the sports person, just as there is for anybody playing in the game of life—the actions of friends or family, coaches or teammates, the environmental conditions, memories, delays and irrelevant thoughts. All of these can distract your focus. Having the ability to focus and be in the correct frame of mind is the key to succeeding in life and consistently producing results.

A classic example of how emotions can affect sport performers came in a famous boxing match between Sugar Ray Leonard and Roberto Duran. Leonard was considered the better boxer and was expected to outclass Duran with slick movements and long-range punching. However, before the fight Duran insulted Leonard in front of his family. To the dismay of Leonard's trainer, Angelo Dundee, Leonard went into a rage. This completely altered the course of subsequent events. Instead of fighting to the pre-planned strategy devised with his trainer, Leonard let his emotions take over and decided he was going to "beat up" his opponent. Duran's actions amounted to a psychological masterstroke as Leonard ditched his boxing skills and opted for a brawl. It was exactly what Duran had hoped for, and he won on a points decision.

ANCHORING

A strategy I have used with many business people, sports people, people looking to find motivation and confidence at the right time is Anchoring. It is an NLP-based technique which can be used to get anyone into the right state of mind.

Regardless of who you are and what you do, there are going to be times in your life when you encounter distractions and challenges. You need to be in the right frame of mind to deal with situations. You can change your state of mind or mood in an instant by using the Anchoring technique. You can stay calm during an interview, relax during a meeting, be confident during a presentation, or be motivated to exercise after a hard day. Whatever is going on around you or however provocative a situation may be, you can stay focused and be in the right frame of mind.

What is Anchoring?

An Anchor is a stimulus that creates a response either in you or another person. When an individual is at the peak of an experience, such as when they are in an intense emotional state, an applied specific stimulus can establish a neurological link between the emotional state and the stimulus. Anchoring can occur naturally or be set up intentionally and can assist in gaining access to a past state and linking the past state to the present and future. Anchoring can be used in sports, business, and personal development. It can be used to create a resourceful state of mind for a specific situation to achieve a desired result.

NLP Anchoring was one of the techniques I introduced to the Blackburn Rovers football club coaching staff in November 2006. I recall speaking to the sports scientist at the time, Tony Strudwick (now at Manchester United). He asked me to deliver some NLP Techniques to the coaches. Anchoring was one of the techniques I introduced to the staff, which included Mark Hughes. The strategies seemed to be well received and to have played their part in a turn-around for the club. They had lost the best part of seven matches prior to me coming in, but thereafter went on a winning run and made the FA Cup semi finals.

Examples of Events That Can Be Used to Develop an Anchor

- Flicking through an old family photo album stirs pleasant memories and brings back feelings associated with them.
- Hearing an old song brings back specific events or memories.
- The smell of freshly baked apple pies reminds you of happy, carefree times during your childhood.
- The smell of sunscreen reminds you of a relaxing holiday.
- Reminiscing about the past with an old friend reminds you of happy times.
- Driving past your old school reminds you of good friends.
- A compliment reminds you of the times when someone gave you a pat on your back.

How We Anchor and Are Anchored

When you are with another person who experiences some strong emotion, whatever you are doing or saying becomes associated with the emotion the other person is feeling. Usually this process occurs at the unconscious level. Subsequently, whenever you do or say the same thing in the same way in the other person's presence, you will tend to re-stimulate some portion of the previous feeling.

Being aware of this phenomenon through the knowledge of Neuro Linguistic Programming enables you to be aware of the kinds of responses you are Anchoring in others and how you are doing it. This also helps you to understand what kinds of responses are being Anchored in yourself and how it is done. This awareness enables you to Anchor for productive outcomes.

How I Have Used Anchoring

Example 1: I was working with a leading football striker who was not performing well because he had spent time off the field injured. He was quickly losing confidence in his abilities. I told him that he had performed well before and he could perform well again. It was just a question of getting him in the same state of mind as when he was playing well. I decided to create an Anchor with the use of technology.

The player's position in the team was to score goals. I found video footage of the player performing to the best of his ability. I transferred as many of these past goals as possible, and there were quite a few, to a DVD. I then created a soundtrack to accompany the images of successful goals using some of the player's favourite music and included that on the DVD. Initially, I asked the player to play the DVD and watch himself playing well.

After he had done that a few times, I then told the player that we needed to develop an Anchor in order to transfer what he was watching to an actual game situation. It needed to be something that could be switched on at will, like a light switch. The player decided he could create an Anchor by flicking his wrist band. Whilst watching the DVD, we went through the Anchoring process hundreds of times until the player knew for certain that the Anchor produced the emotional stimulus required for him to perform well. The result was that in the player's first game, he scored two goals and went on to have his best season ever.

Example 2: I worked with another football striker at a lower division club. The player was lacking in confidence. Although he was performing well in practice and had no trouble scoring goals, whenever he walked on to the football pitch, he didn't believe in himself and was unable to score a goal.

I didn't think it was necessary to find out the reasons behind this problem, what was needed was to find a solution. In this situation I did not have access to video footage of the player, so we created the Anchor by getting the player to reflect on some of his past successful performances. I asked him to sit and write down some of his best performances. Whilst he was doing this, you could see an immediate physiological change. He sat up straight, his breathing changed, and almost in an instant he was in a different mindset.

Once again, we decided on a flick of his wrist band to create the Anchor. Every time he flicked the band, I asked him to visualise his best performances. Soon, every time he flicked his wrist band, he tapped into the feeling of making a successful goal. He performed the technique and practiced whilst on his own.

The first thing he does now when he walks on to the pitch is flick his wrist band. This has created a positive impact on his performances, helping him to become one of the Team's and League's top players.

Example 3: I have also developed team anchors. I was working with a football team that was struggling. They were at the bottom of the league and headed for relegation. This time I used a huddle to create an Anchor. I played a DVD of their best performances. After they had watched it a few times, I asked them to form a huddle and visualise themselves playing as they had done on the DVD. I wanted them to associate the huddle with the same level of application and effort for each game. The result? The team went on to win 8 out of the next 10 games and survived relegation against all odds. Every game they played after developing the Anchor was outstanding.

Example 4: The Accrington Stanley football team had problems. They were second from the bottom in the relegation zone and on a losing streak. They were also under the threat of a points deduction due to allegations of fielding unregistered players in a game. My guess is all this had a psychological effect on some of the player's minds.

Chris, another NLP therapist, had approached Accrington before the end of the previous season about doing some work with the team. I had spoken to Chris about this and remembered thinking it would be a good opportunity for her to test her skills in football. I gave Chris a call about working with me to turn the Accrington team around, and the rest, as they say, is history.

We went to the club on the first day, spoke to the management team, and had a word with the players. This helped us to solidify our ideas about what we wanted to do. We began by showing the team some DVDs of their best performances of the season, closely monitoring what they had done. We then went through some NLP techniques they could use—Anchoring, positive language, visualisation, creating a compelling future, etc.

The session went well. After the consultations, Chris and I decided that it would be especially helpful to tie the NLP to some physical sessions. The next day we put the players through what I call a "speed agility quickness session" and integrated it with NLP. I told the players to make sure the ball hit the back of the net during a goal as often as possible. I Anchored it verbally with words such as, "finish, hit the target, and well done." I told the players that every time they saw a scoring opportunity, to think of hitting the back of the net with the ball. I tapped them on the shoulder after they had scored; in effect, covering all representational systems in Anchoring.

Chris took them through a "brain gym" during the training sessions. On the Friday before the game, she guided them through some NLP. In football, the key is to win, and the first game we had a resounding 3.0 win.

That set the tone for things to come. During the next seven weeks we Anchored and used NLP at every opportunity, focusing on getting the team to play to the best of their ability. The team won the next 5 out of 7 matches, only losing by one goal both times. Accrington also won 4.1 against Grimsby and in the decisive game against Macclesfield, they won 3.2. This last game was important because it meant the club was mathematically safe.

It was a great experience and a fantastic opportunity to work with a great bunch of lads and a great management team. Of course, much of credit goes to Chris, who showed great spirit, particularly because she was recovering from a knee operation. To come into a situation like that for her first major role with a football team was a real baptism of fire.

It was fantastic having another NLP practitioner to bounce off ideas and act as a sounding board. The lads and staff really took to her, just as I knew they would.

Installing an Anchor Exercise

1. Decide on a specific event you wish to access with a particular state of mind (confidence, motivation) for matches, presentations, interviews, and meetings.

2. Decide on the state you want to Anchor—being calm and relaxed, confident, motivated, etc.

3. Choose an Anchor(s) that will trigger that state; e.g., press thumb and middle finger together, flick wrist band, etc.

4. Recall a memory or imagine a situation where you experienced that state, a situation in which you were totally calm, relaxed, confident, etc. Fully associate to that memory or feeling. Close your eyes and notice what you saw, felt, and heard.

5. When the memory is vivid and you have experienced it through to the peak of its intensity, squeeze your thumb and middle finger together, flick your wrist band. etc.

6. Release the Anchors when the experience begins to fade.

7. Do something else; e.g., open your eyes and count down from 10 to 1 to break the state and distract yourself.

8. Repeat the steps above several times, each time trying to make the memory even more vivid. This step is not required when the Anchor was established at the high point of a real experience; if it was completely virtual, you can strengthen the Anchor by establishing it at the high point of several such remembered experiences.

9. Apply the Anchor and check that the required state occurs.

10. Project into the future and imagine your forthcoming event and using your Anchor.

Keys to Anchoring

Intensity of the experience: An anchor should be applied when you are fully associated in an intense state. The more intense the experience, the better the anchor will connect.

Timing of the Anchor: When you reach the beginning of the state, apply the Anchor. When you reach its peak, let go of the Anchor. This can vary typically from five to fifteen seconds. For example, if you want to Anchor confidence and are reliving a time when you felt the confidence you want, apply the Anchor as soon as you first have the feeling of confidence and release it just as you reach the peak of the feeling.

Stack the Anchor: The Anchor has to be repeated and reinforced in the same way from time to time. So, every time you receive praise or recognition, stack your Anchor to reinforce the positive feelings.

Repeat: The more often you repeat the stimulus, the more powerful will be the Anchor. If you keep adding, or stacking, Anchors, it becomes even more powerful.

You now have a powerful technique to help you get the best out of yourself in any situation.

NLP Physiology Strategy

Have you ever come across a person who trudges around with the head down and back hunched and who talks slowly? Have you ever come across a person that walks with purpose, head up and shoulders back and a sense of direction?

Many years ago, I was that first person. When I was growing up, I lacked confidence. I didn't excel at school, and, because I matured very late physically, I was small in height and struggled to compete with my peers in sports. I would try to hide with my head down and back hunched to avoid being pushed around. Even when I grew to over six feet in height, I still trudged around with my head down. It wasn't until I learnt an NLP technique called Walk with Grace and Power, that I worked with my posture and experienced a transformation in confidence.

One of the points I stress with the athletes, sports people, and footballers I work with is to adopt a confident, positive posture. Whether they are standing with the opposition in the tunnel getting ready to walk onto the pitch or have given everything on a sports field with a few minutes to go, I tell them they must keep a positive, confident posture.

Example 1: A few years ago I was working with a professional footballer who was on an opposing team to the one I was currently helping. He said that at half time he felt physically knackered even if the game was a thrilling encounter. During a match between his team and the other one I was helping, his team walked onto the pitch for the second half. He saw the other team standing tall, shoulders back, heads up. He said his team was literally beaten at that point.

Example 2: I was in Sydney Australia delivering seminars. I hadn't been back to Australia in many years, even though it was where I was born and grew up. I wasn't sure how the audience would respond to my seminars. There was a little bit

Picture yourself as a student and your teacher walks into the classroom with purpose. Imagine you are interviewing someone who walked in with shoulders back. Envision someone stepping up to deliver a presentation with a self assurance. What would your impressions be?

of uncertainty in my mind. Because the seminars were well publicised on the radio and the papers, the crowd was large. I found myself hunching over and ducking my head. When I was ready to stand up, I remembered that the best way to get into the right state of mind is to walk out with a sense of purpose, head up and shoulders back. This I did. The seminars went down like a storm.

By changing the way you move your body, you can have a subtle but important influence on the way you feel. Here's a quick experiment to illustrate this point:

1. Try to feel depressed as you jump up and down and shake your hands in the air.

2. Try to feel confident as you slump your shoulders and look down.

3. Try to feel tired and listless as you march around the room.

Changing your physiology is probably the simplest way to change your state of mind in an instant. The following technique is something you can practise for a few minutes each day to help change your state of mind:

Step 1: Stand up straight in front of a mirror.

Step 2: Put your shoulders back and hold your head high.

Step 3: Stand in that position for 1 minute.

Step 4: Walk in that position by pacing in place.

Step 5: Whilst pacing in your position of power and confidence, focus on five of your best qualities.

Notice how you begin to feel after even one minute. When you perfect this technique, it is something that will occur naturally and give you a sense of pride in who you are.

Chapter 11

Modelling Excellence

"Champions do not become champions when they win the event, but in the hours, weeks, months and years they spend preparing for it. The victorious performance itself is merely the demonstration of their championship character"

—T. Alan Armstrong

One of the most efficient ways to help you achieve your goals in sports or life and to become the best you can be, is to find someone who has achieved what you are aiming for. If you learn what they did to get to that point, this process will save you a lot of time and provide valuable insights. If you were going to run a marathon for the first time, would you ask for advice from someone who has run one before or from someone who hasn't?

THE DIFFERENCE THAT MAKES THE DIFFERENCE

We all have a brain which has exceptional capabilities; if one person has the capability of doing something, then so can someone else. How many young swimmers were inspired by Mark Spitz? Football players by Pelé? Young boxers by Muhammad Ali? Basketball players by Michael Jordan?

How did Christiano Ronaldo become one of the best footballers in the world? How did Michael Phelps becomes one of the greatest swimmers of all time? How did Sir Richard Branson become one of the world's most successful entrepreneurs?

The one question I like to ask successful people is who and what inspired them. Even as a child, I have always enjoyed hearing people tell me who had been the inspiration behind their success.

Role models are people who influence our lives. Particularly in our childhood, role models have a big impact on our lives. We are, in essence, a product of the people we decide to model. Sometimes it can have a positive effect on our life and sometimes a negative effect.

I was at a coaching award ceremony once where I had been nominated for a coaching award. The guest speaker was an Olympic swimming medallist. In his speech he talked about how, at an early age, he saw an Olympic athlete dressed in full Olympic regalia and it inspired him to want to be the same. It was that moment that was the spark of inspiration that would transform his life.

> Possible for you, possible for me; it's just a matter of how.

Time for Reflection

Everyone has been influenced by other people in their life. If you are a parent, have you said the same things to your children your parents said to you? If you are an athlete, who was the person who inspired you to play your sport? Throughout your life, whose behaviour have you modelled, who have been the people you have modelled? It could be a parent, a friend, a teacher, or a sports hero.

Exercise

- Who were the sports people in your life that had the most impact?
- How have they influenced you?
- What are some of the things that have served you from adopting their behaviour and some of the things that haven't?

Life is about timing. If we meet the right person under the right circumstances at the right time, it opens up many possibilities. However, we don't need to leave things so much to chance. There are plenty of people out there we can learn from if we have something we would like to achieve, skills and capabilities we would like to learn, or resources we would like to acquire.

Learning from people who have mastered a skill and who are getting results gives us an amazing and powerful insight. It also makes us realise we are all human. We all make mistakes. If one person can get into their best shape ever, so can someone else. If one person can take an excellent free kick, hit a golf ball, run a marathon, be a successful coach, be happy and confident, then so can someone else.

Modelling involves identifying people, teams, or organisations that are excellent and figuring out what precisely it is that they do. Even more important is how they do it when they are "being excellent." Excellent behaviour comes from a level of unconscious competence, what are often referred to as "habits." When someone is "being excellent" they are not thinking about what they are doing, they simply do it!

For example, have you ever played a perfect game of golf, tennis, or football, made a "hot" tennis serve, played out of your skin, or been "in the zone?" You didn't have to think about what you did, you just did it. That is operating out of the unconscious. You barely even notice time, everything flows.

Talent is learnt, not inherited! What we take to be natural ability is actually a set of values, beliefs, and unconscious behaviours that have been learnt, perhaps by chance, and then reinforced by subsequent experience. So, if you have the desire, you can become all you wish to be!

Exercise

Write down all the things you are capable of (1) technically, such as serving a tennis ball, taking a free kick, performing a skill, and (2) behaviourally, such as confidence honesty, exhibiting a belief, or performing a task.

+ When did you learn the capability?
+ How did you learn the capability?

Modelling for Excellence in Business, Sports, and Life

The first step in the NLP modelling process is to identify an expert and to elicit the underlying values and beliefs that relate to the expert. Then map the "strategies" that they used, the actual steps in thinking and acting that they perform. If you are looking to improve your golf swing, find someone who has an excellent technique. If you are looking to be more confident, find someone who is confident. If you are looking to improve taking a free kick, find someone who is excellent at taking free kicks. You get the idea.

In a physical skill, the mental state is crucial to making the muscles act together in the desired sequence in order to kick a ball for a goal, hit a devastating return in tennis, or run a marathon in record time. In an interpersonal skill, the mental state will also be reflected in external behaviour. This time, though, it is language, tonality, pace, gestures, posture, breathing, facial expression, etc., to which others unconsciously respond.

Modelling excellence has been at the heart of my work, from modelling top flight athletes to successful businesses people—the people who are getting results in different aspects of their life. I have even modelled people and organisations that were not successful and compared them to successful strategies and noticed the difference. On many occasions, this difference was minimal. Sometimes mere millimetres separated the top and the mediocre. By employing modelling, someone achieving average results could improve beyond belief.

When I first starting working with football club youth teams, my aim was to put together a programme to help develop players to their full potential. I searched for a template or templates I could use.

I first looked at the Manchester United football club. They had been producing world-class players such as Ryan Giggs, Paul Scholes, and David Beckham, to name a few. It was one of the biggest clubs at the time and had resources I could only dream of. However, I believed it was possible to learn what they were doing in training and use some of their methods and techniques.

A few of the other teams and organisations I looked at were the Australian Institute of Sport, Ajax football club, and the Crewe football club. I wanted a large range of variation because my youth teams didn't have the resources and infrastructure of the bigger clubs and many of the smaller clubs didn't have the psychological mindset. Through modelling, I elicited some key strategies.

I told my young players that the first thing I was introducing was a fitness test. I had been fortunate to obtain the fitness test results of a Premier League team. I set my players a goal of achieving the same levels of fitness. Because football is a physical sport and statistically a player only touches the ball for approximately 3 minutes in a 90 minute game, the value of being in top shape is immense.

I told them that if a top player can run 3,500 metres in 12 minutes and run the 20-metre sprint in less than 3 seconds, these were their targets. For a player to know that physically they are as fit to participate in football as the leading players would give them a massive psychological boost.

However, physical ability is not the be all and end all. Other key components are technique, tactics, belief, confidence, and other psychological resources, all of which can be modelled.

So a template of excellence was created by combining the attributes of several different clubs—what their fitness levels were, what they were doing technically and tactically, even what they were eating. Even more important, what was going through the mind of these high-level players? What did they believe about themselves and their teammates? How did they walk, talk, think and feel?

My goal was to get into the mind of the best footballers and transfer that attitude to my players. I knew the average number of players that graduated from youth team football and go on to play professionally was around ten percent. I wanted to smash that.

Some of the players who came out of my program were Colin Kazim Richards, Nicky Adams, David Worrall, and many others. As a result of raising the bar and replicating excellence, even on a tight budget and scarce resources, this program produced champions.

I have used this same principle with other sporting infrastructures, athletes, business people, and sales representatives, and with people looking to get in shape, develop positive character traits, improve the quality of their life, and take a positive step forward.

Jimmy uses modelling to help develop his young players to their fullest potential.

Behavioural modelling is the study of what accounts for the results that people achieve. It can be used to discover the key components of thinking, feeling and behaving that someone at the top of their field experiences. We can all learn from people who are achieving what it is we are aiming to achieve.

Behavioural Modelling

The Structure of Experience

All of what we experience in life is comprised of various elements: behaviour, emotions, patterns of thinking, and the beliefs or assumptions on which those patterns are based. Differences in experiences are a direct result of differences in how these elements are structured. That is, your behaviours, what you are feeling, what you are thinking, what you believe, and how all of these elements interact with one another, combine to give rise to your experience at a moment in time. That array of content and relationships constitutes the structure of the experience.

It is within these structures that we find the differences that distinguish someone who is adept from someone who is not. In modelling, we are "mapping" out the underlying structure of experience that makes it possible for someone who is excellent in their field to manifest his or her particular ability. If we structure our experience to match that of the person who is excellent in their field, that structure will enable us to manifest (to a great extent) that same ability.

Modelling, then, is the process of creating useful "maps" (descriptions of the structure of experience) of human abilities. Such maps are useful because they allow us to understand the experiential structure that makes it possible for a person to manifest a particular ability. Such maps are useful because they can make it possible for anyone to have that experience or ability by making those maps their own.

Once you find a positive role model, you need to work out what they are doing differently from you. You need to look at how they do what they do. For example, what do they do when they are taking a free kick in football, communicating effectively as a coach, performing a specific sports technique or skill, or delivering a tactical presentation to a sports team? Watch their physiology carefully whilst they perform the task.

Studying just the physical element isn't enough. You also need to find out what is going through their mind to support their ability. You need to find out by asking searching questions about what the experts are thinking and saying to themselves when they are performing at their best. (If you actually get the chance to ask them directly, that's even better.) Once you have defined your successful model, then you can transfer their skills and capabilities to yourself.

I remember when the successful football manager Jose Mourinho first started working in the UK Premier Leagues. During a press conference he called himself "The Special One." Whilst many people were taken by surprise by the comment, I knew this was a belief that had obviously had a positive impact on his career as a football manager. There were many other coaches who had as much knowledge as Jose Mourinho; after all, he wasn't recognised for his playing ability. He had never played football at a level anywhere near that of many other coaches. At one point he was actually working as a translator for a football manager.

No doubt he had worked hard to get to where he was and achieve his success. Many other people had worked equally as hard, if not harder, but had never achieved his level of success. Was it his belief that made the difference? We'll never know, though I am sure it didn't do him any harm.

Understanding the Modelling Process

Each of us has a particular set of strategies that enable us to function effectively whilst performing skills and capabilities such as driving, cooking, playing sports, delivering a presentation, working in business, and a thousand other functions. These skills are most often acquired by unconscious trial and error. For example, when you first learnt to drive, your instructor taught you when and how to change gears, the rules of the road, and how to steer. There may have been times you stalled the car, crunched the gears, or drove too slowly. With experience, you almost never do those things anymore. Through your own experiences, you've learnt and acquired skills in sports or business throughout your life. However, you have little idea of how to transfer them to others.

When you ask people who are really excellent how they do what they do, the most common response is, "I don't really know," or "I just...sort of...do it." This is typical of "unconscious competence."

Even a little modelling will show that people often use widely different internal processing strategies. This accounts for the gap between the mediocre and top performers. Once most strategies are made explicit, they can be easily learnt or modified to accomplish team or personal goals. By the end of the modelling project, the person being modelled invariably says, "Well, I never realised that's what I do." Often they will add, "I thought everyone did it that way!"

Implementing the Key Steps

1. Imagine being the expert that you identified who has the behaviour, skills, or abilities that you want for yourself.

2. Close your eyes and visualise that person in action. Watch it like a movie in your mind. See how they look, how they how use their body, how they use their posture; how they stand, walk, and sit. Pay close attention. Hear how they talk, what they say, and how they say it.

3. For each expert, gather information with respect to what and how she or he is thinking, feeling, believing and doing when manifesting the ability.

4. Use contrast and comparison of examples to identify the essential structural patterns for each expert.

5. Use contrast and comparison of examples to identify the essential structural patterns for each ability.

6. Step into the role model's place and see yourself conducting this choice of behaviour, skill, or capability. You are watching yourself do as the model does. You have taken over the role and are acting exactly like your role model.

7. Do you feel any negativity come up within you when you watch yourself? Do you have any doubts that you are capable of doing the skill

or capability? Go through the actions of the skill and adjust your action in the movie until you are happy with how you perform and feel positive and confident in your abilities.

8. Mentally step inside the picture. You are now inside your movie looking through your own eyes. You are no longer watching yourself. You are doing the skill and capability just the model did it. How does it feel to perform this skill or capability or be this person with these new skills and capabilities? How does your body feel? How is your posture? What do you hear? How does your voice sound to you?

9. Imagine a future situation where you want to implement these skills and capabilities. Put yourself there. Look through your own eyes at this situation. You are the star of this movie and behaving in a new way! Is it all working? Do you need to make any adjustments?

10. Open your eyes and come to the present moment.

11. Imagine that you are now the new you with these new capabilities. Get up and walk around as the new model. Walk the walk and talk the talk, as they say. How does it feel?

12. Notice any insights this gives you and immediately write down these insights.

13. Test and refine the model.

I am not suggesting that you should become a copy of your expert. You will always keep your own unique identity as there is only one "you" in the world. This is simply an opportunity to imagine being your expert. It can benefit and assist you in learning how they did it and implement some of their strategies to help you on your path to success.

The Technique

Review the key points discussed in Implementing the Key Steps. Make out a list of questions you would ask your expert if you could. For example:

1. Who was your inspiration?

2. How did they inspire you?

3. Where and when do your perform your skill or capability?

4. What specifically do you do?

5. If you were going to teach me to do it, what would you ask me to do?

6. How did you learn to do this?

7. What do you believe about yourself when you do this?

8. Do you have a personal mission or vision when you do this?

9. How do you know you are good at this?

10. What emotional and physical state are you in when you do this?

11. What happened for you to be good at this?

12. What are you aiming to achieve when you're doing this?

13. Who else do you recommend I talk to about this?

Ask yourself these same questions and compare your answers to the ones you "received" from the model. Decide what you can take from the model to boost and enhance your capabilities in a specific area.

Of course, it is more useful if you can actually ask the questions in an interview. You may be surprised who would respond to you if you make the effort to contact your expert model. It never hurts to ask.

If you're finding it difficult to obtain access to the person(s) you're looking to model, read through interviews in magazines or on the internet and glean as much information as possible to answer your questions. The answers you find may give you invaluable insight into you own mindset. It only takes one piece of information to make a difference to your life.

Your model expert didn't wake up one morning and have a great golf swing, excellent communication skills, or an excellent free kick. They worked at it. They practiced both physically and mentally, they hired coaches or trainers, they developed a plan. You too can do all of these things.

The power of modelling is immense. To conclude this chapter, I will share a time when I was working with a team of aspiring young professional football players.

One of the players, who was short in stature, felt that this might be a factor holding him back in his career. Height seemed to be important in the position and league in which he was playing.

I had once read an autobiography by Roy Keane, one of the greatest midfielders of his generation. I recalled he mentioned something about his height at a key point in his career. I told the young player to read the book.

He read the book and told me it had helped him overcome beliefs about his height and how it was hindering his professional career. It was a turning point and he would go on to become an outstanding professional. He had told me that if Roy Keane could do it, so could he.

Chapter 12

Peak Performance

"Champions aren't made in gyms. Champions are made
rom something they have deep inside—a desire, a dream, a vision."
—Muhammad Ali

Every athlete, performer, or sports person, at some point in their career, has succumbed to pressure.

Thousands of people play a sport for the thrill of having fun with others who share the same interest. For others, it's not always fun and games. There can be a ton of pressure on athletes from high school through to semi pro and the pro game. A lot of the time it can come from the athlete's feelings that a parent or coach always expects them to win. This can of stressful expectation can also come from a group of supporters, from a town right through to a nation.

As their career progresses, athletes and performers may face many negative and harmful effects because of increased competition and pressure. They must often perform in situations where the intensity and stress levels become very challenging. When this occurs, athletes, coaches and parents need to know effective strategies to help athletes and performers deal with pressure in sports.

We have all seen footballers miss a penalty. Do you remember when Robert Baggio, voted one of the world's best soccer players, missed the target completely from the penalty spot against Brazil in the 1994 World Cup Final? It was a moment when stress and pressure won because his strategies for dealing with them were momentarily forgotten.

It is one thing to be playing snooker in your local club when you're relaxed and in your zone. It's a totally different environment if you're playing in the 1985 Snooker Final, you've been going for 14 hours, and you're aware that 18.5 million viewers have turned on their television to see if you mess up and lose the game. The difference between an amateur and a true professional is whether they thrive under this kind of pressure or if the emotional stress causes them to crack.

How do athletes deal with pressure? It is different for everyone, but one of the best methods I have found is EmoTrance.

EmoTrance is a technique developed by Dr Silvia Hartmann. It gives techniques that help people deal with many kinds of stress and pressure, such as public performances or athletic competition, in order that they can process the increased energy.

Imagine stepping out from the tunnel at Wembley and having 90,000 eyes staring at you, 90,000 people cheering, clapping or even booing. Where do you feel the "energy" of this situation in your body?

Close your eyes and imagine stepping up to take a penalty that will win or lose the match for your team. All eyes are on you. You can hear your supporters cheering and feel your enemies willing you to fail. Where do you feel that "energy" in your body?

It is important to not only practise your technique over and over until it becomes completely natural, you'll also need to develop your mental technique for achieving peak public performance in the high energy sporting arena.

Using the EmoTrance system, there are two ways of handling this incoming energy:

1. Learn to shield yourself from it so that nothing touches you and you are left in the calm centre of the hurricane around you. When this happens, the energy from those thousands of eyes just bounce off you, like rocks against a shield, and you feel calm and still inside. Unfortunately, this is a short-term fix that often leads to people snapping or breaking, like Wayne Rooney did when he had a go at fans for his own dismal performance during the 2010 World Cup. Think of your shield like the levees protecting New Orleans from hurricanes. They work fine until a critical point is reached and at that point, the city behind them is decimated.

2. Allow the energy from the crowd to rush through your body like flood waters through a storm drain. Feel energised, alive and ready to achieve anything. However, all incoming energy should have an exit point, so practice feeling the energy coming in, flowing through you, and going out. The entry and exit points are personal to you, so don't force it out the base of your feet if that's not where it wants to go.

Using and practising EmoTrance techniques can help you harness the energy in the arena to your advantage and stay calm and cool, like Roger Federer does at Wimbledon when hitting the winning ball at match point.

Chapter 13

Relaxation

"Every now and then, go away and have a little relaxation, for when you come back to your work your judgment will be surer. Go some distance away because then the work appears smaller and more of it can be taken in at a glance and a lack of harmony and proportion is more readily seen."

—Leonardo Da Vinci

Could you imagine living in a world without television, mobile phones, computers, the internet, no deadlines at work, no need to be at a certain place at a certain time? Whilst there are many benefits to modern technology and the modern world we live in, the one thing we are probably all guilty of is not giving ourselves the opportunity to unwind. By unwinding I am not just referring to an annual holiday, which sometimes can be a stressful adventure in itself. How many of us take the opportunity to switch off and relax, meditate, and kick back on a daily basis?

TIME OUT

Unlike our ancestors, we live with constant stress. Instead of occasional, acute demands followed by rest, we're constantly over-worked, under-nourished, exposed to environmental toxins, worrying about others, working long hours, and placing more demands on ourselves—with no let-up. A certain level of stress is fine because it can motivate us to do things, but high levels of stress can damage your health by producing high levels of cortisol in the body. Studies and research have proven that by adopting relaxation strategies, we can bring down our levels of cortisol, improve our well being, and bring down our heart rate and blood pressure.

What is cortisol? Cortisol* is an important hormone in the body, secreted by the adrenal glands and is involved in:

+ proper glucose metabolism,

+ regulation of blood pressure,

+ insulin release for blood sugar maintenance,

---

* Cortisol: a stress-related hormone that decreases the immune response. Athletes who train too hard are breaking down muscle and cortisol will impede the body's ability to repair muscles, making athletes more likely to get injured or to exacerbate a chronic injury.

- immune function, and
- inflammatory response.

In its normal function, cortisol helps us meet these challenges by converting proteins into energy, releasing glycogen and counteracting inflammation. Small increases of cortisol can help us get into action on Monday morning, get our brain in gear before an exam, give us a burst of energy when we are tired, and lower sensitivity to pain if we have an accident.

For a short time, higher cortisol levels are okay. But at sustained high levels, cortisol gradually tears down your body. It destroys healthy muscle and bone, slows down healing and normal cell regeneration, co-opts the biochemicals needed to make other vital hormones, impairs digestion, metabolism and mental function, interferes with healthy endocrine function, weakens your immune system, and can lead to heart disease.

Just think of your body's response when you watch a scary film, when you receive some bad news, when you're frightened, upset, or embarrassed. Your heart beats faster, your palms get clammy, your stomach gets tingly. This is the body's ancient "fight or flight" response to perceived threat or danger. During this reaction, certain hormones like adrenalin and cortisol are released. Technology may have evolved, but our human responses have not. Fight or flight is now activated in situations where neither response is appropriate, like in a traffic jam or during a stressful day at work. When the perceived threat is gone, our systems are designed to return to normal function via the relaxation response, but in our times of chronic stress, this often doesn't happen enough, causing damage to the body.

A University of Connecticut study in 2004 confirmed that soccer players with elevated levels of cortisol from stress and inappropriate training experienced reductions of performance during a season.

The most consistent psychological factor related to sports performance and injury from competition and training seems to be stress. It follows that the ability to cope with stress can act as an essential buffer to reduce the likelihood of injury. Although the causes of stress can reside both inside and outside the sporting arena, and the coping mechanisms used by athletes may vary; one of the fundamental buffers to stress is controlling the level of cortisol your body naturally secretes when it is under stress.

When physical and mental stresses exceed the level of physiological adaptation (training), the body's internal systems cannot proceed efficiently. Sports training schedules are based on the phenomenon that the best time to begin the next training session is only after there has been sufficient period of rest. If training occurs too often, while the body has not yet compensated for former expenditures of energy, there is a decrease in the level of physiological performance resulting in the phenomenon of overtraining.

Therefore, the use of adaptogens* in sports is connected mainly to the fast increase of physiological adaptation (level of training) due to accelerating the anabolic (regenerative) metabolism processes. This accelerated regeneration results in an increase in energy and maintenance of specific protective systems in the body.

Improving the functional maintenance of body systems with the help of adaptogens produces an increased level of physiological adaptation resulting in improved focus, stamina, endurance and recovery. Use of adaptogens during trainings and directly before competition has been confirmed in a number of international studies.

To keep cortisol levels healthy and under control, the body's relaxation response should be activated after the fight or flight response occurs. During a stressful day at work, when you feel overwhelmed or upset, take time out to recharge your batteries. Lifestyle changes—so you're not always facing stressful situations—are beneficial.

Relaxation and Meditation

If you want to decrease stress and lower your cortisol, taking time out each day to relax and meditate may be the solution. Considerable scientific evidence has established that relaxation and meditation techniques are valuable therapeutics for optimal health.

An article in Psychoneuroendocrinology highlighted meditation's effects on levels of various hormones, including cortisol, in otherwise healthy male subjects who were subjected to mental and physical stressors (Psychoneuroendocrinology, vol 29). In this randomized study, blood samples were taken and hormone levels analyzed at the study's onset and again four months later after the subjects had learnt and practiced a meditation technique. Those who had practiced meditation had lower average cortisol levels compared to subjects who had not meditated, suggesting that meditation may help reverse the effects of chronic stress.

A paper in the journal, Psychosomatic Medicine, described how women with stage I or II breast cancer could decrease their perceived levels of stress, as well as their cortisol levels, by simple cognitive-behavioural, stress-management techniques (Psychosomatic Medicine, vol 30).

Stress Management and Relaxation

One mental skill that is fundamental to developing further mental skills is stress management. This includes facets of emotional control. Participation in sports can

---

* Adaptogen: natural herb products that increase the body's resistance to stress, trauma, anxiety, and fatigue.

lead to a number of different emotional responses, such as the feeling of anxiety. Some athletes are aware when they feel stressed—rapid heartbeat, butterflies in the stomach, sweaty palms—while others are unaware of these signs. The first key to stress management is to help the athletes identify their emotional responses to stress.

When athletes learn how they typically respond to stress, they are better prepared to intervene proactively to reduce the effect stress may have on performance. This is accomplished by teaching athletes various stress-management techniques to teach the athlete three things: (1) to control their mental–emotional states associated with athletic performance, (2) to learn which emotional states are associated with superior performances, and (3) to learn how to program future responses for performance.

This teaching involves the use of various relaxation techniques. This can involve progressive relaxation, breath control, meditation, or imagery. All of which are designed to help an athlete learn how to notice signs of tension within the muscles.

Another area related to this topic is the teaching of excitation techniques, methods designed to help athletes bring out activating emotions for improved performance. Several methods can be taught to help accomplish this goal. These techniques include the use of cue words or phrases to remind athletes of the importance of the situation or practice. Imagery can also be used, such as the athlete imagining that they are about to perform in a major competition.

Why the emphasis on getting the athlete into an optimal emotional state? Many sport psychology professionals believe that the odds of an athlete performing at their best are greater when they are in this state than when they are not (Robazza, Bortoli, Zadro, & Nougier, 1998). Through observation and interviews and assessment, a sport psychologist can identify an athlete's optimal emotional state and then teach them how to recreate this state during performance.

Hypnosis techniques have long been used by golfing professionals, but the therapy has now become more popular in other sports, including football, rowing, boxing and cricket. Sports men and women are increasingly aware of the benefits hypnosis can bring to improving their performance alongside other methods, such as sports psychology.

Relaxation Exercise

The following relaxation exercise is one I use with the athletes and business people I work with to help them relax after stressful times in their lives. Stress reduction not only brings health benefits, but also improved performance, feeling sharper and more focused, and feeling positive.

To show my clients the physiological power of relaxation, I ask them to take their pulse rate for one minute. After the relaxation exercise I ask them to retake their

> Tiger Woods displays the brilliance of Hypnotherapy.
> He has acknowledged that he uses hypnotherapy before every game he plays
> to help calm his mind and improve his focus.

pulse. They find that their pulse rate has dropped, sometimes by up to 20 beats per minute. Twenty beats may not sound like much, but if you think about how many minutes there are in a day times 20, that's thousands of beats less strain per day on your heart.

So, take your heart rate before the script by finding your pulse on your wrist or on your neck and count the beats per minute. At the end of the relaxation strategy, take your pulse rate again and notice the difference.

You can record the following script and play it back to yourself with relaxing music playing in the back ground.

Relaxation Before Visualisation

Close your eyes, take a deep breath in and a deep breath out. Imagine emptying all your thoughts into a bag and putting it aside in a place where you can pick it up later if you wish.

Imagine visiting a place where you feel completely relaxed and at ease. It could be an amazing beach, a relaxing country walk, or lying back on a yacht that is sailing on a beautiful river or crystal-clear ocean.

You feel happy, secure, and loved. It's a warm, beautiful summer day and the sky is a clear shade of blue. You feel a gentle breeze on your face.

The sun is shining brightly. You close your eyes and feel the warmth of the sun on your body. Then the warmth spreads to your shoulders and arms. You begin to relax even deeper.

The warmth is moving into your hands, relaxing all those muscles. You feel at ease and peaceful.

The warmth of the sun moves gently into your thighs, into your calf muscles, and finally into your feet. The warmth of the sun releases tension and stress and every muscle in your legs is so relaxed that you feel at peace with the world.

As you breathe in, you inhale crystal clear relaxing air. As you exhale, you release all your stresses and strains. As you hear yourself breathing and you feel your heart beating, you become more and more relaxed.

Your whole body is now totally and completely relaxed, from the top of your head to the tips of your toes. As your body relaxes, so does your mind. Notice the sun going down, going down and down, deeper and deeper. The sky is ablaze with an abundance of colours of crimson and bright purple and yellow streaks. It's a beautiful summer evening. Your mind relaxes and lets go, releases all the stresses of the day. You feel safe. secure, at peace. You seize the moment and take it all in, picking up a refreshing drink, refreshing every part of your body.

As you watch the sun go down, the sky changes to a clear, deep blue with millions of stars twinkling in the night sky. You notice one particular shining star. You focus completely on that star. Nothing else matters except this beautiful solitary, sparkling star in the sky. It's a beautiful summer's night. You feel so safe, secure, so comfortable, relaxed, happy and at peace with the Universe.

Imagine yourself now, floating towards that star in the sky, moving up and up and up. Your body is weightless as it lifts up to the star, going higher and higher, up and up. As you look down you see all the bright lights shining below. You can see all your family and friends happy and relaxed. You are completely at ease. You now float to within touching distance of the star. You reach out and become the star and the star is you. You go deeper and deeper into a relaxed state. Just let your minds go. You are at peace, calm, happy, and relaxed. Let your mind and body experience the joy of pure relaxation at the deepest level.

When you are ready to come back, do so gradually on a slow count of five.

> 5—gradually coming round
>
> 4—feeling refreshed and relaxed
>
> 3—feeling recharged and revitalised
>
> 2—feeling rejuvenated, relaxed, and recharged
>
> 1—back to the here and now

You are completely refreshed, relaxed, recharged and energised with an understanding of your life's path and purpose.

Chapter 14

Power of Visualisation and Imagery

"I've discovered that numerous peak performers use the skills of mental rehearsal and visualization. They mentally run through important events before they happen."
—Charles A. Garfield

The human mind can not distinguish between reality and non-reality. Have you ever had a bad dream and woken up with your heart racing? Have you ever watched a scary film that made you break out in a cold sweat?

Athletes use visualisation, complete with images, of a previous best performance or a future desired outcome to focus on how they want the outcome of a competition or training session to go. They use it to keep calm before the nerves of a big event kick in or to wind down afterward when the adrenalin has been pumping. This helps the athlete stay relaxed, focused and confident.

Research has found that visualisation can have a big effect on performance. Visualisation and imagery can give the athlete the confidence to perform certain skills under high pressure situations. The most effective visualisation involve a very vivid experience in which the athlete has complete control over a successful performance.

In a study at the University of Chicago, researchers carried out experiments into visualisation in basketball players. They divided the players into three groups and tested each group as they took numerous penalty shots. The groups were then given different instructions:

+ Group 1 did not practice penalty shots for 30 days.
+ Group 2 practiced penalty shots every day for 30 days.
+ Group 3 practiced penalty shots only in their mind (visualisation) for 30 days.

After the end of 30 days, the three groups were tested again:

+ Group 1 showed no improvement at all (as expected).
+ Group 2 showed a 24% improvement (not especially satisfactory given that they had been practicing with the ball for an entire month).
+ Group 3 improved by 23% (impressive, considering they had not even seen a ball for an entire month!).

Visualisation can be used to prepare for a big match, overcome stressful or anxious situations, and build confidence. With mental rehearsal, minds and bodies become trained to actually perform the skill imagined and give best possible chance to achieve an outcome.

In sports, visualisation can include any of the five senses: visual (sight), kinaesthetic (feelings), auditory (hearing), olfactory (smell), or gustatory (taste). Using the mind, athletes call up these images over and over, enhancing the skill through repetition or rehearsal in a manner similar to physical practice. Visualisation can be used for anybody looking to focus on a positive outcome in their sport.

HOW WE VISUALISE

Let's get a better understanding of how the process works by using one of the key aspects, or what we call sub-modalities in NLP.

What are Modalities and Sub-Modalities?

We process and learn information through our five basic senses or modalities. For each of these modalities, we can have finer distinctions, or sub-modalities that define the qualities of our internal representations. A picture could be described as being black and white or colour, or it could also be bright or dim. Sounds could be loud or soft, or coming from a particular direction. Feelings could be in different parts of the body or have different temperatures. Smells could be pleasant or offensive, strong or light. Taste could be sweet or bitter or strong or mild. Most people work with only three modalities—visual, auditory, and kinaesthetic. However olfactory or gustatory sub-modalities can play an important role in a person's ability to associate an experience.

The visual sub-modality of Associated–Dissociated is very important and refers to whether or not you can see yourself in the picture (visual internal representation). You are associated if you do not visualise yourself as being in the picture but instead as though you are actually experiencing the event. Often we refer to this as "looking through your own eyes." If you can visualise yourself in the picture, as though you were watching yourself in a movie or a TV show in which you have a role, then we say you are dissociated.

If you are associated in a memory, then your feelings (happy, sad, and fearful) about that memory will be more intense. If you are dissociated, this is more like watching a movie of your life rather than being there (on the playing field) and any feelings will be less intense.

Some of the more common sub-modalities are:

Visual	Auditory	Kinaesthetic
Black and White or Colour	Loud or Soft	Strong or Weak
Near or Far	Near or Far	Large Area or Small Area
Bright or Dim	Internal or External	Weight: Heavy or Light
Location	Location	Location
Size of Picture	Stereo or Mono	Texture: Smooth or Rough
Associated–Dissociated	Fast or Slow	Constant or Intermittent
Focused–Defocused	High or Low Pitch	Temperature: Hot or Cold
Framed–Unbounded	Verbal or Tonal	Size
Movie–Still	Rhythm	Shape
If a Movie: Fast/Normal/Slow	Clarity	Pressure
3-Dimensional or Flat	Pauses	Vibration

Sub-Modalities: Key Building Blocks of NLP Techniques

I recall discussing a sprinter's preparation for the 100 metres. He mentioned that whenever he was in the lead at around the 80-metre mark, he would surrender the lead. He said when he was in the lead and got to 80 metres, he would imagine ten foot figures running behind him, could hear big foot steps, and breathing down his neck. This sub-modality would cost him the race.

If he "came from behind," this sub-modality would disappear.

Sub-modalities are key components to many of the NLP techniques employed in making changes. They have been used to assist people to stop smoking, eat more of certain foods and less of others, address compulsion issues, change beliefs and values, enhance motivation, move from stress to relaxation, address phobias, etc.

In order to change an internal image, feeling, or voice that limits you in some way, then:

+ change the colour of the image,
+ push the image away,
+ release some of the negative feelings,
+ turn down the volume,
+ make it more pleasant, and
+ make it appear farther away.

At some point, the house you live in, the car you drive, the phone you use, all originated in someone's imagination. Our mind is capable of producing both positive and negative thoughts and images and translating them into reality.

Imagery and Visualisation

Your thoughts have a direct influence on the way you feel and behave. If you tend to dwell on sad or negative thoughts, you most likely are not a very happy person.

Your imagination can be a powerful tool to help you combat stress, tension, and anxiety and focus on what you want. You can use visualisation to harness the energy of your imagination. It can have an effect right away. The more you do it the better you will get at using visualisation and imagery to help you overcome life's challenges.

Visualisation Exercises

The following exercises illustrate how sub-modalities work. Close your eyes and think of a recent experience; e.g., driving in to work, walking to the shop. Notice any images in your mind (an internal representation). For some people, the pictures are very clear. For others, the picture won't be as clear. This is why it is important whilst we use imagery to use as many senses as possible which will help create a stronger association.

Exercise 1: Get in a comfortable position. Close your eyes and get a picture in your mind of a pleasant experience; e.g., a holiday or family meal. When you have created this picture, notice the sub-modalities. Is it bright or dim? What feelings are you experiencing? Can you hear any sounds such as music or conversations? Do you smell anything, such as the smell of the ocean and beach or sunscreen. Do you have any tastes, such as ice cream or fresh lobster? Are the sights, sounds, and feelings associated as though you are living them, or dissociated as though you are watching it on TV. Once you have done this, open your eyes and clear your mind of that experience by stretching and looking around the room.

Exercise 2: Get in a comfortable position. Close your eyes and this time get a picture in your mind of a mildly unpleasant experience. Notice the sub-modalities. What do you see, hear, feel, smell and taste? Can you identify several sub-modalities in this mildly unpleasant experience that are different from the picture of the enjoyable experience? Once you have done this, clear your focus by stretching and looking around the room.

It's a good bet that you were able to identify several sub-modalities that were different in the two internal representations. Generally, you will tend to have similar sub-modalities for the internal representations for pleasant experiences. The sub-modalities of the internal representations of unpleasant experiences will also be similar and in some ways different from the sub-modalities of pleasant experiences. This sameness and difference in sub-modalities allows us to code our experiences and give meaning to our past and future memories (internal representations).

Exercise 3: Did you notice the proximity to you of the experiences in Exercises 1 and 2? Were they large or up close ("in your face")? If the experience was unpleasant and in your face, what do you think would happen if you made the picture smaller and pushed it away to a comfortable distance? Usually, that makes the intensity of the experience less significant.

Exercise 4: Close your eyes and think of a time when your game was great—you played exceptionally well and felt fantastic. Once you have this picture, make it very dark, shrink it down to a small picture and push it far away. When you did this, what did you notice about your feelings of the game? Were they minimised or did they disappear? You have just learnt a great way to remove your ability to perform in a match—take all your memories of good performances and make the pictures very dark, small and far away. Of course, I am joking. However, there are some people who tend to discount their best performances by making them darker, smaller and further away, whilst making their worst performances big and bright and close. How do you think that affects their game?

Exercises 3 and 4 illustrate that the sub-modalities you use to store your memories are what give meaning to your memories. You can not change an event that has already happened. However, by adjusting the sub-modalities of the memory, you can change how you perceive it and respond to it. This is also true for future events.

Imagery Can Involve Negative Visualisation

Unfortunately, many of the images popping into our heads do more harm than good. In fact, the most common type of imagery is worry, but what we worry about exists only in our imaginations.

It is estimated that, on average, people have 10,000 thoughts or images flashing through their mind each day. At least half of those thoughts are negative, such as anxiety about winning a match, scoring a goal, missing a put, etc. Unharnessed, a steady dose of worry and other negative images can alter your physiology and make you more susceptible to negative performances in your sport.

Your thoughts have a direct influence on the way you feel and behave. If you tend to dwell on sad or negative thoughts, you are more likely to feel negative. Likewise, if you think that your sports performances are enough to give you a headache, you probably will come home with throbbing temples each day. This is just another clear example of the power the mind exerts over the body.

If you can learn to direct and control the images in your head, you can help increase your effectiveness in sport. Imagination is like a spirited, powerful horse. If it's untamed, it can be dangerous and run over you. But if you learn to use your imagination in a way that is purposeful and directed, to tame the horse, so to speak, it can be a tremendously powerful vehicle to get you where you want to go.

Your imagination can be a powerful tool to help you combat tension and anxiety. You can use visualisation to harness the energy of your imagination. It does not take long—probably just a few weeks—to master the technique. Try to visualise two or three times a day. Most people find it easiest to do in bed in the morning and at night before falling asleep, though with practice you'll be able to visualise whenever and wherever the need arises.

How Effective is Imagery?

Imagery has been found to be very effective for athletes. Imagery is at the centre of relaxation techniques designed to release brain chemicals that act as your body's natural brain tranquilizers, lowering blood pressure, heart rate, and anxiety levels. By and large, researchers have found that these techniques work because they relax the body.

I have found that visualisation works best when it is used in conjunction with a relaxation technique. When your physical body is relaxed, you don't need to be in such conscious control of your mind. You can give it the freedom to daydream. Just sit back and relax and let everything go. Whenever you need to relax, return to the Relaxation Before Visualisation exercise in chapter 12. Once you feel comfortable in your favourite scene, gradually focus your mind to an event you want to rehearse.

Focusing on what you want helps you to work towards your outcome.

Preparing Your Body for Visualisation

Before you begin visualisation, sit or lie down in a comfortable position and close your eyes. Just let everything go and completely relax. Relax every part of your body.

+ Flex and relax your toes.
+ Flex and relax your ankles.
+ Tense your calves, release and relax
+ Flex the muscles at the front of your legs (quads) and at the back of your legs (hamstrings), tense and relax.

- Tense and relax in succession your core muscles, working through the lower back, stomach, chest, and shoulders.
- Tense and relax your neck muscles.
- Tense and relax your facial muscles and your eyes.
- Inhale and exhale gently. Imagine breathing out stress in the form of black smoke and breathing in a relaxing, clear energy.
- Relax your mind. As you relax your mind, imagine emptying all your thoughts into a bag. You can pick up your thoughts later at any time, but for right now just let them go. Once you feel relaxed, think of a time when you felt happy, peaceful, calm, and in tune with the world. Imagine every aspect of the time: the place, people, sounds, colours, and feelings. Involve all of your senses. You are now at peace and in tune with the world, open to opportunities.

It is important to use all the five senses. For example, if you like to visualise the ocean, first imagine what it looks like: the swell of the waves moving in until they are crashing on the shore, the size and movement of the waves, the sky above, and the sun sparkling on the ocean. Then imagine the smell of the sea. Next, listen for the sounds the waves crashing on the shore, children laughing and playing in the distance, the breeze blows, birds singing. How does the sand feel beneath your feet? Is it soft and smooth and warm? Is the sun gentle on your back? Is the breeze blowing softly on your face? Imagine you are quenching your thirst with a cool drink.

As you become more involved in your visual image, your body will relax and you will be able to let go of the problems or worries you felt before. To encourage this relaxation to occur, you can punctuate the images with positive statements, such as "I feel loved and secure" or "I feel calm and relaxed."

Additional Scripts

Following are some imagery scripts to assist you with your sport, prepare for a press conference, or talk to your team.

Public Speaking

Choose a comfortable position, seated or lying down. Make sure that you have no distractions around you and are not trying to do anything besides focusing on these words and allowing yourself to become relaxed.

- Prepare your body for visualisation.
- Take a deep breath in…and breathe out.
- In and out.

- Continue to breathe deeply, slowly, and comfortably.
- Count down from 10 to 1. As you count each number, you become more relaxed.

    10 let your muscles start to relax

    9 warmth starts at the tips of your toes and spreads gently up through your body

    8 your muscles are becoming more and more relaxed

    7 notice your mind drifting, becoming more relaxed

    6 you are relaxing even further now, letting everything go, feeling peaceful

    5 a warm feeling of relaxation and love spreads through your body

    4 you are becoming more and more relaxed and peaceful, tranquil

    3 free your mind and feel it relax

    2 you are feeling completely relaxed

    1 you are now in a state of deep relaxation; comfortable, loved, secure and happy.

- Allow this feeling of relaxation to grow, becoming even more relaxed, calm and peaceful.
- Keep with you this feeling of relaxation, love and security as you think about public speaking. Notice your reaction, physically and emotionally, to the concept of public speaking. Perhaps in the past this has been a source of anxiety for you. Notice now how you can be relaxed, peaceful, calm and confident while thinking about speaking in public.
- In the future, you will find that the feelings you used to associate with stress symptoms you will now associate with excitement. This is a positive feeling, filling you with energy. The thought of speaking in front of people fills you with good feelings of excitement and anticipation.

- You may even be feeling a bit excited now, just thinking about public speaking. Let this feeling subside as you return to a state of deep relaxation.
- Take a deep breath in. Hold it and exhale.
- Breathe in and out.
- In…out
- Continue to breathe deeply; noticing how you relax a bit more each time you exhale.
- Breathe in…breathe out and relax.
- In…out…relax.
- Keep breathing slowly and calmly. You can relax like this any time you need to. Whenever you want to calm down, you can breathe deeply, and relax just like you are relaxing now.
- (Pause)
- Now let's begin a guided imagery exercise to allow you imagine successfully speaking in public and enjoying the positive experience. Visualise everything going perfectly and see yourself as the most confident, best public speaker in the world.
- Create an image in your mind of an excellent public speaker. Imagine a confident, well spoken person. See that this person is you. Picture yourself as a superb public speaker.
- Begin to create a mental picture of yourself preparing to give a speech. You are feeling confident and excited. You're looking forward to speaking.
- After your focused preparation, you are ready to speak. When the day arrives, you are excited, eager to begin.
- Imagine going to the location where you will speak. See yourself looking forward to speaking. You are excited, eager to talk in public. You can't wait to share your knowledge. You have memorized the words and know that they will come to you exactly as you need them.
- Picture entering the location where you will speak. People are gathered to see you. You love it. They can't wait to hear what you are going to say and you can't wait to tell them.
- Imagine getting up to the front of the room, ready to speak. The crowd waits expectantly.

+ Picture all the details of this scene. See yourself standing at the front of the room, feeling confident. See the people in front of you, waiting to hear you speak.

+ Imagine yourself beginning your speech, confident that your phrases and words are well timed. All throughout your speech, you breathe calmly, deeply, pausing between each sentence. You maintain a comfortable, smooth rhythm. Your speech is smooth and clear. Ideas flow. Your hard work and extensive preparation allow your public speaking to be easy, automatic, and almost rote. Everything seems so familiar. It is such a great feeling.

+ Imagine giving your speech. See yourself as you enjoy this moment. You are confident, comfortable, and having a great time. The anticipatory excitement you felt at the beginning has smoothed into a feeling of confidence and calm.

+ You feel so at home in front of all these people. They listen and enjoy hearing you speak as much as you enjoy speaking. You take pleasure in this experience immensely.

+ When you reach your conclusion, and speak the final words of your prepared speech, the audience responds with enthusiastic applause. Imagine giving the audience time to ask questions. You answer every question easily and proficiently. See your excellent answers satisfying each member of the audience.

+ The audience is pleased with your performance. You are pleased with your performance. The exhilaration at having completed this public speaking fills you with happiness, contentment, and pride. Notice how fantastic it feels to have shared your unique knowledge with this group of people.

+ Notice how you can feel confident and calm when doing public speaking. This includes giving prepared speeches and responding to questions. The words flow and you are skilled and able to do any sort of public speaking. You are able to relax before, during, or after you speak. You are confident and assertive.

Practicing this visualisation in your mind is like performing the actual public speaking. If you are able to do this visualisation and be calm, you can also speak calmly in public. Congratulate yourself for completing this challenge.

Now that you have completed this public speaking guided imagery, take a few moments to reawaken your mind and body, gradually becoming more alert.

- Count to five. When you reach 5, you will be fully awake and feeling calm and energized. Confident in the knowledge you're special and unique and have the ability to speak to audiences successfully and confidentially.

  1 become more awake and alert

  2 feeling your mind and body reawaken

  3 move your muscles a little

  4 almost completely awake now

  5 feeling full of energy and refreshed, recharged, and positive.

Relaxing After a Match

Find a position, seated or lying down, where you are comfortable and can relax. You might want to close your eyes or focus your gaze on one spot in the room.

- Take a deep breath in, filling your lungs. Breathe out, emptying your lungs completely.
- Breathe in again through your nose. Breathe out through your mouth.
- Breathe in and out.
- In…out.
- Keep breathing slowly like this, fully emptying your lungs with each breath.
- Your deep breathing calms and relaxes you, allowing your body to relax.
- This is your time to relax, enjoying this time to yourself. You enjoy being totally relaxed. You deserve this time. You need this time to function at your best. This time of relaxation will allow you to be as calm and healthy as possible. Appreciate yourself for who you are. This relaxation is providing your mind and body the time it needs to balance itself in a productive, healthy way. You are looking after your health and well being. Letting everything go, emptying all your thoughts
- As you continue to breathe slowly and comfortably, turn your attention to your body. Notice how you are feeling physically. Simply become aware of the sensations in your body. You can hear and feel your breathing, your heart beating. You are feeling pleasantly relaxed.
- Imagine completely relaxing every part of your body, beginning at the top of your head, release any tension. As you breathe deeply you are relaxing deeper and deeper. Move downward. Focus on your eyes, nose, and chin, breathing deeply, releasing tension, and feeling more and more relaxed.

- Move down to your shoulders and release any tension. Noticing how your body feels more and more relaxed.
- Keep moving down your body. Release any tension from your chest muscles. Feel more and more relaxed.
- Release any tension from your stomach muscles.
- Release any tension from your hips, becoming more and more relaxed.
- Release any tension in your knees.
- Release any tension from you legs all the way down to your feet.
- Take a moment to notice how your body feels to be relaxed from the top of your head to the tips of your toes. You have released any tension from all your muscles, joints, and bones. You feel warm and relaxed.
- Notice where your body is the most relaxed. How does the relaxation feel? Imagine that this relaxation is warm and soothing—growing... spreading—relaxing other parts of your body.
- Find the spot of greatest relaxation and let it grow to every part of your body. Feel your body becoming more relaxed as it does so.
- Imagine that the air you breath in is pure relaxation. Imagine that the carbon dioxide you breathe out is tension. The air exchange is an efficient relaxation system. Feel the relaxation as you take it in through your nose and relax your body, adding to the area of relaxation already there. Expel your body's tension, breathing it out through your mouth.
- Continue to exchange tension and relaxation. Continue the generalized anxiety relaxation exercise.
- Feel the relaxed area getting bigger as you breathe more and more relaxation into your body. Breathe out tension and feel the tension getting smaller.
- Breathe in relaxation and breathe out tension.
- Each breath in adds to the relaxation. Each breath out diminishes any tension.
- Keep breathing in relaxation and breathing out tension. You grow more and more relaxed with each breath.
- (Pause)
- Soon the areas of tension are very small. Your breathing can eliminate them entirely. Imagine breathing out any last bit of tension.
- You are feeling so calm, so relaxed that there is no tension left. Now you both breathe in relaxation and breathe out relaxation.

- Breathe in…relax
- Breathe out…relax
- Keep breathing smoothly and regularly, relaxing more and more deeply with each breath.
- You are now completely relaxed, calm, and at peace
- Feel your feet and hands grow warm. Feel the warmth as it moves from your feet up through your legs. Feel the warmth in the core of your body as the warmth moves from your hands and through your arms. The warmth from your arms and legs meet at your stomach. Feel your core growing warm and relaxed.
- Enjoy the feeling of relaxation throughout your body. Simply rest, enjoying this relaxation. Floating…relaxing.
- Focus now on your thoughts. Notice how calm your thoughts are. You enjoy this mental relaxation.
- Let your mind relax and wander. As your mind wanders, notice how peaceful you feel.
- Now, simply allow your mind to drift. You don't need to focus on anything at all. Just rest and relax, enjoying this pleasant state you are in.
- Keep relaxing for a while longer, enjoying this pleasant, calm feeling. Enjoy the feelings of relaxation.
- When you're ready, gradually reawaken and come back to the here and now.

Sit quietly for a moment with your eyes open, reorienting yourself to your surroundings. Stretch if you want to, allowing your body to reawaken fully.

When you are fully awake and alert, you can return to your usual activities, feeling wonderful.

A Good Night's Sleep

What is important for any athlete or coach is to get a good night's sleep in the lead up to a sports event. This guided relaxation will help you fall into a deep, restful sleep in the days before a match or the night after the match when adrenaline is keeping you awake.

- Begin by lying on your back, placing your hands in a surrender position. You can change positions any time you need to in order to be more comfortable, but start by lying on your back for now.
- Mentally scan your body for areas of tension. Take note of how your body feels. During this sleep relaxation session, you will focus on releasing any

tension in your body and on quieting the mind. Once the mind is calm and peaceful, you will easily drift into pleasant, restful sleep.

- Breathe in, drawing in life-giving air and relaxation.
- Exhale slowly, expelling any tension.
- You might have thoughts about things you did today or things you need to do tomorrow. Perhaps you are worried about something or someone. Just imagine emptying all your thoughts into a bag, knowing you can pick the bag up in the morning and revisit your thoughts if you wish
- Now is the time to clear your mind for sleep so tomorrow you will be refreshed and ready for a new day, totally refreshed and positive about the tasks you have throughout the day.
- Now take a few moments to think about a pleasant experience in your life, reliving the pleasant experience like its happening in the here and now. Notice what you heard, felt, and saw, focusing on the pleasant experience. For the next few minutes, relax and relive this pleasant experience.
- Really relax and enjoy this time, feeling totally relaxed, calm, and at peace.
- Notice how your body feels right now.
- Where in your body is today's tension stored? Focus your attention on the part of your body that feels most tense. Focus in on one small area of tension. Breathe in deeply and then let that tension go as you breathe out.
- Notice where your body feels most relaxed. Let that feeling of relaxation grow with each breath, gradually spreading the feeling of relaxation throughout your body.
- Feel your attention drifting as you become sleepy and calm. For the next few moments, count slowly from 1 to 10, focusing on counting in a relaxing, calm, peaceful voice. As you count, you will become more deeply relaxed. As you relax, you can allow your mind to drift into pleasant, refreshing sleep. Concentrate just on the numbers.

    1 Fill your body with relaxation.

    2 You are more deeply relaxed...deeper and deeper...calm, peaceful.

    3 Feel the tension leaving your body and relaxation filling your body and mind.

4 You are now very relaxed and calm. There is a tingly feeling of relaxation in your arms and legs. They are very heavy...pleasantly heavy and relaxed.

5 As you drift deeper and deeper, you can feel calm and sleep washing over you. You are peaceful.

6 You are deeply relaxed.

7 Your body and mind are very calm.

8 You feel so very pleasant and heavy.

9 Allow your mind to drift...easily...no direction...floating...relaxing.

10 You are deeply relaxed.

+ Now, slowly count backwards from 10 to 1. Focus only on the numbers and with each number you'll begin to feel more relaxed

10 You are nestled in deep relaxation.

9 You are warm...heavy...peaceful...comfortable.

8 You feel pleasant and calm.

7 You are drifting.

6 You are letting go of everything.

5 You feel at peace with yourself.

4 You feel very sleepy...deeply relaxed.

3 You are drifting toward a deep sleep that will give your body time to revitalise.

2 You feel completely relaxed, calm and at peace with the world.

1 You are feeling warm and calm, fully relaxed, as you drift into a deep sleep.

+ Relaxed...peaceful...drifting into deep sleep...deep pleasant sleep...sleep.

Visualising for Sports

The Basic Picture

Outline the basic content of a match or a technique to be imagined. Write it down in the first person (I). To describe a skill execution, make sure you include all components of the skill to be imagined or behaviours to be emphasised, especially if it is a complex skill such as taking a free kick, kicking for a goal, serving at tennis, making a golf swing, making a snooker shot. If you are describing the events in a sport situation, include all actions that occur in the event and the correct sequencing of all the actions.

Describe the technique in step-by-step details. Include your role on your team, and your game plan.

Adding Details

Use your senses to fully associate to the experience—describe any colours, sounds, and feelings. Describe the environment; e.g., context and weather. Describe any movement qualities such as speed or direction. Add the kinaesthetic feelings, physiological or body responses, and the emotional responses. The words that are added are action words that clearly describe the quality of actions or emotions.

Refine the Script

Read it to yourself and imagine the event in all its sensory, action, and emotional detail. Do you feel as if you are actually executing the skill or experiencing the event? If not, re-examine the descriptors and action words to see if they accurately reflect the sensations associated with this action.

Tape It

When you have a suitable script, record it onto audiotape. You can then use it as a prompt for your imagery training.

Example Recording for a Free Kick in Football

Basic Story Components: Describe your preparation, the football, the players around you, the goal posts, the goal keeper, and anything else you can think of.

Technique: Look at your target. Move into the ball on an angle, keeping your head down, foot moving toward the ball and pointing in the direction you want the ball to go. Arms out for balance, head down, and strike.

Adding Detail: See the ball on the grass and the distance to the goal. Hear the crowds. Look at the point on the goal where you want to direct the ball. See the position of the goal keeper.

Script for Striking the Ball

- I am feeling completely relaxed and confident.
- I feel the grass under my feet.
- I see the ball clearly on the grass.
- I focus on where I want the ball to go into the goal
- I move into the correct position in order to strike the ball.

- I am moving towards the ball on an angle.
- I feel the power and timing in my body.
- I feel my foot striking against the ball in exactly the spot I want to strike it.
- I feel my body in the correct position for following through from the strike.
- I watch the ball leave my foot and travel over the wall, travelling past the keeper, right toward the corner I was aiming for.
- The ball hits the back of the net and I feel the excitement of scoring a goal.

Imagery can be used in any situation where you want to focus on a specific outcome or for any technical aspect of any sport; e.g., golf swing, snooker shot, tennis serve. Imagery puts you in the driver's seat, giving you the opportunity to create an outcome you want, giving you the best possible chance to succeed in your task.

Imagery is exactly what you make of it. Guided imagery is not mind control. It is a process we do automatically. However, rather than leaving things to chance or letting your mind control you, the visualisation process actually gives control back to you so you can make conscious what had been an unconscious process that influenced you.

Imagery techniques allow for personal changes by changing and growing with you. The more adept you become at image exploration, the stronger your unconscious mind grows and the more pathways you have at your command.

Chapter 15

Proximity

"Attitude is a little thing that makes a big difference."

—Winston Churchill

Your network is the net worth of the people with whom you associate and represents who you are emotionally, intellectually, and financially. The same applies in sports. If the people you train with are positive, you're more likely to be positive. If you train with people who are negative, you're more than likely to be negative.

Have you ever been in a good mood and feeling optimistic about the way you are playing and performing? Then someone you know phones and speaks negatively? You hang up feeling negative. Perhaps you have experienced this situation the other way around. You have been having a hard time finding form as an athlete and a few words of encouragement from someone makes you feel better and more optimistic.

Exercise

+ Write a list of all the people you train and participate with in your sport with during the week.
+ List the people who have a negative effect.
+ List the people who have a positive effect.

Minimise the time you spend and train with people that have a negative effect on your life. Misery is always looking for a new breeding ground and some people drain energy from you. These people always moan and complain, telling you how it's impossible to play at the highest level; they are negative and miserable.

These are the type of people you only hear from when they want something from you or when things aren't going well in their life but about which they never do anything to change. They don't have the initiative to do the hard training in order to get the best out of themselves. They have lost the passion of playing their sport.

Stay away from them.

Spend more time with people who have a positive effect on your life. Associate with people who are looking to train hard and have similar aspirations to you. Make the effort to meet as many of these people as possible because they will have a positive effect.

Of course, there will be times when normally positive teammates are going through hard times and you want to be there for them, and vice versa. You will have a special bond with certain teammates and have a special bond with certain friends; however you have the choice. Your career will soon be over and the people with whom you associate will have a major impact on your life, helping or hindering you.

It amazes me how often people tell their problems to others who can't do anything for them anyway. They go into training and moan about things to someone else on the team who has similar problems, and then they go home and moan about their team to their partner, who doesn't have personal knowledge about their sport. Sometimes you have to accept that they may not be the best person to give you advice on certain subjects.

If you listen to people repeatedly run over the same old ground, you are not doing them any favours. Sometimes it's worth pointing people toward professional help. After all, if someone wasn't feeling well, you wouldn't diagnose them. You would advise them to see their GP! To a certain extent, the same principle applies to many aspects of sports. There are many top professionals out there, like personal trainers for fitness, nutritionists, relationship coaches, career advisors, etc, who have the knowledge required to help people. If someone isn't happy in the place they are in, they need to do something about it. Be wary of being dragged in, as there is only so much support you can give before you become emotionally drained yourself.

Chapter 16

Laughter

*"Life does not cease to be funny when people die any more than
it ceases to be serious when people laugh."*

—George Bernard Shaw

Have you ever been on a night out with your teammates, been on an away trip, or had some banter in the training ground, and you laughed so much you could barely breathe? Didn't it make you feel great? One of the best tonics in the world is laughter and having a good laugh is free.

So much money is spent on professional sports these days. Sports have become a major business with merchandise and TV rights. Footballers are becoming millionaires at 20 years of age. Everyone seems to have forgotten that, on the face of it, sports matter so little.

If you a burdening yourself with a sense of expectation and pressure and forget the purity and enjoyment of the game, it is harder to find form than when you are enjoying your sport and feel relaxed.

One of the best resources you have is your sense of humour.

Laughter makes you feel good and that feeling remains with you even after the laughter subsides. Humour helps you keep a positive, optimistic outlook through difficult situations, disappointments, challenges and losses in sports. Laughter strengthens your immune system, boost your energy, diminish pain, and protect you from the damaging effects of stress. Best of all, this priceless tonic is fun, free, and easy to use.

If you haven't already watched the film Patch Adams, staring Robin Williams, make an effort to find a copy. Patch Adams was a doctor who would dress up as a clown to entertain seriously ill patients, having a positive effect on their life. Adams' ability to make people laugh lifted the spirits of seriously ill patients around the world.

You or your team might be going through a hard time, or you might be thinking it isn't always easy to laugh with the expectations and pressures of sports. It is possible! Here are some tips and exercises you can do which can assist you in instilling a more positive outlook on life so you can immediately start to feel better.

+ **Smile.** A simple smile can light up a room. Get into the habit of smiling
    and sharing a smile with the people around you, walking on to the
    training ground with a smile, and playing your sport with a smile.

- **Create a Gratitude List.** Write a list of all the things you are grateful to have in your life. Some of the things we can often take for granted, such as food, clothes, access to technology, family, friends, being alive.
- **Laugh.** Spend time with people who enjoy having a laugh. Have you ever spent time with people who are negative and walked away feeling drained? Spending time with people who enjoy having a laugh is infectious and makes you feel better.
- **Find the humour.** Integrate humour into your conversations at the training ground and with your teammates. Some of the best leaders, teachers, coaches, and influential people are people who use humour to get a point across or ease tension. The positive effects of sharing a joke and seeing the funny side of life is a great way to build rapport and make people feel at ease.

Create opportunities to laugh.

- Go for a good night out with your teammates
- Watch a funny film.
- Go to a comedy show.
- Read a funny book.
- Spend time with funny people.
- Share a good joke or a funny story.
- Do something fun that is out of the ordinary.
- Make time for team-building activities outside of your sport.

Attempt to Laugh at Challenging Situations. Look for the humour in a bad situation. Look for something positive to come out of something negative. Put things into perspective; there are so many bad things happening in the world but at least you can remember to enjoy your sport.

Lighten Up. Let go of the things that you can't control and focus on your life. Being able to laugh at yourself is an art in itself so do it often; sometimes it's easy to take yourself too seriously. Look at the bright side of your sport.

Keep Things in Perspective. Some of the things we worry about are unimportant on the big scale of things. There is no point in getting worked up or being upset about things that don't really matter in the big picture.

Remember It's All Temporary. Sometimes it's worth drawing on past challenges and realising everything—whether good or bad—is temporary. Strive to keep a positive outlook good in every situation. It's not always easy to laugh; however, when facing adversity, being able to dust yourself off, put a smile on your face, roll up your sleeves, and have a good laugh is often the best way forward.

Letting Go of the Past

"Getting over a painful experience is much like crossing monkey bars.
You have to let go at some point in order to move forward."

—Author Unknown

Playing sports is truly an amazing journey. You have probably heard the saying, "Life is what you make it." Playing sports is what you make it also. Sports bond people together and capture the imagination of people of all ages. The one thing for certain in sports, as in life, is that no one knows how long they have. If you knew how long your career was going to be, what would you do differently?

Have you ever come across sports people who constantly go on about things in the past being a major factor in being able to move forward? The story of their past weighs them down like the weight of the earth of on their shoulders.

Imagine going back in time to the beginning when you played sports with enthusiasm and pure enjoyment. A time when you spent countless hours kicking a ball about in the back garden with your mum calling you in for tea. Your thoughts and feelings about the game you love are fresh. The game begins; you are on a journey of life and sports. It is from that moment that the person you are takes shape.

The nature vs. nurture debate will always rumble on. Maybe the person you develop into came from a combination of both. One thing is for sure—along the way you develop emotions to certain events and actions that have an impact on your life. You don't have to be a rocket scientist to work out if you had bad experiences participating in your sport—a negative coach, you didn't receive encouragement from your family, or you were told you were crap at sports and a useless idiot, particularly by people you looked up to—you potentially could develop negative emotions about the way you participate in sports or how you feel about yourself.

When you watch television or read magazines, you are told you are supposed to live in a certain way and do certain things. It may be type of car you should drive, the type of house you should live in, the furniture you should have, your hair, clothes, body shape and size; the list goes on. If you don't conform to what's considered the "norm," you're left feeling inadequate.

The same applies in sports. You see pictures of your favourite stars on magazines and watch them on television. Without really considering how they got to where they

> You have read this book this far. You have a little further to go
> and then you will embark on your own special journey.

were or the reality of who they are as a person, you see them as role models and feel let down if they are revealed as anything less in the media.

The truth: none of us are perfect. We are human and we live and learn and make mistakes along the way. Some people continue to live their life based on one experience. It only takes one negative comment or one bad experience and it's taken on board as a belief without the person even stopping to question the validity or rationality of the comment or experience.

I once had a client who had lost their enthusiasm to play sports when it should have been the peak of his career. He said he felt worthless. He felt that if it wasn't for his ability to play sports, he would have no one. He thought it might have been because of the constant negativity he faced that came from the people around him when he was trying to succeed in sports from an early age.

It is sad the things people say and do to other people. Sometimes I work with a person who has grown up under the most difficult of circumstances and suffered physical or verbal abuse. Or both. It can make it difficult for them to move on. People can sabotage their life on many different levels—personally, professionally, in relationships—with feeling of inadequacy. There comes a time, if they are going to move forward, when they need to let go of emotions tying them down to the past.

CLEARING UP NEGATIVE EMOTIONS.

I once used this technique with a footballer who had a fear of failing in competitive games. He played well in training but would freeze in matches. He had an important game coming up and had to play because some of his teammates had been injured. He was feeling anxious and nervous. He was a very talented player, with excellent ability; however, the prospect of playing a big game made him extremely nervous.

It turns out he was associating with negative emotions he had experienced many years earlier when he was in his early primary school years. A teacher would subject the students to humiliation if they got a question wrong by getting them to stand in the front of the classroom and explain their answer.

He was not born with these negative feelings. He had developed associations to this experience and they were going to detrimentally affect his life if he didn't do something about it. We worked with the Releasing Negative Emotions technique, which benefitted him greatly.

Another time I was working with a lady who had initially entered my programme to lose weight. Having achieved that goal, she mentioned she had a phobia of swimming and she had tried everything to overcome it. She mentioned a bad experience she had had at a swimming pool when she was 8 years old. She was now 64 years of age and hadn't been in a swimming pool for 56 years. She was living her life based on an experience that happened all those years ago. Whatever she tried to do to overcome these feelings had not worked.

Where swimming was concerned, she was living her life as though she was still eight years old. She wasn't born with this fear. One moment in a swimming pool had stuck in her subconscious and every time she even thought of going for a swim she felt the fear developing.

We did the Releasing Negative Emotions technique and she overcame this fear in less than one hour. She booked some swimming lessons and has been swimming ever since. I have done with technique with many people over many years, helping them overcome negative feelings or attitudes that had been limiting their life.

Releasing Negative Emotions

You need a balloon and a pin for this technique.

+ Identify a negative attitude or a feeling that is preventing you from fulfilling your potential in sports or achieving a goal, an ambition, or a dream.

+ On a piece of paper, write down some significant events that have happened in your past related to your sport, positive and negative; e.g., the first time you scored a goal, had a disagreement with a coach, made the high school team, travelled with a team for first time, a bad game, a good game.

+ Now write done some of the things you're looking forward to in the future; e.g., playing at a higher level, winning trophies, excelling at your sport, getting on an exciting new team, travelling to new places, fans cheering you on.

+ Close your eyes. Relax and imagine a scene with a line stretching off to the right that represents your positive future. Place all the exciting things you're looking forward to doing on the line.

+ Visualize yourself on a short line in the middle of the scene that represents the present.

+ Imagine those past events you wrote down and place them in the scene on a line that stretches off to the left and represents your past.

- Now, join your lines of the past, present and future events.
- Remembering the negative attitude or a feeling you have, imagine going backwards in time, identifying all the times in your past when you had that negative feeling. Make a mental note at each of the times you notice those negative feelings. Continue backwards to the very first experience you had with that attitude or feeling.
- When you reach the very first experience, step off the line and detach yourself from the feeling. Move to the left and look at the memory.
- See your younger self. What happened for you to feel these negative thoughts about yourself and the people around you?
- Next, step to the right and look at the memory from a future perspective.
- Imagine floating above the experience so high you can barely see it.
- Now, float back down and imagine going to a time shortly before the event happened that produced those feelings or attitude. You realise those feelings were not always there. There was a time were you didn't have those negative feelings.
- Gather all the information about what happened each time you felt this way from different perspectives by walking or floating alongside your timeline to the present.
- As you arrive at the present, look back along your timeline of past events to that very first instance when you experienced these negative feeling or attitudes.
- Determine what resources you have at the age you are now—your life experiences, your intelligence, and the wisdom you have gained playing your sport or living your life. What do you see, hear, and feel when you are at your best? What do you know now that would have been useful to you in that negative experience when you were younger? Remember, when you're young, you do the best you can with the knowledge you have at that time. Now that you are older, you know how to deal with those feelings a lot better.
- Imagine filling up a several bags with all the positive resources you have now and bringing them back to your past.
- Imagine walking back alongside your timeline to a place immediately before the memory of the past. Imagine passing a bag with all these resources—your confidence, intelligence, experience, and wisdom—to the person you were when you first had these negative feelings about yourself.

97

- Now, how is your response different to the experience you had that made you feel inadequate or negative? How do you feel differently about yourself?

- Let go of those negative emotions; let them go forever. Your mind works to serve you and it may have been holding these thoughts to protect you, but now it's time to let them go.

- Pick up your balloon and exhale all those negative feelings into a balloon. Blow it up as big as you can. Imagine getting rid of every ounce of the negative feelings or attitude you had. Once you are rid of the negative feelings, tie up the balloon, pick up the pin, and burst those feelings.

- Walk back towards the present. Each time you come across the same negative feelings, replace them with a bag of the positive resources. As you make your way back to the present notice how you feel after having releasing all the negative energy.

- Imagine how you will respond differently to events and interactions with people, your teammates, coaches, and fans, and the effect it will have on your sport.

- Imagine two weeks into the future, then two months, four months, six months, and finally one year into the future laying down a bag of these new positive resources at each point.

- From the future, turn to face the present and notice the changes you have made by letting go of the old, negative feeling and replacing them with those new positive resources. Give your present self whatever information you have that will assist you in making those changes.

- Now, gradually come back into the present feeling positive, refreshed recharged, focused and determined.

Congratulations you have broken free of a negative aspect from your past. Now, for the future.

Chapter 17: Part II

•

The Path We Take

"Do not follow where the path may lead. Go instead
where there is no path and leave a trail."
—Ralph Waldo Emerson

It takes one moment of inspiration to completely transform your career. A great goal, an amazing game, a chance encounter that will help you draw on a new set of opportunities and create a sports career of purpose.

STANDING AT A CROSSROAD

Imagine yourself standing at a crossroad of your career in sports. You have come to a decision point. Do you continue to do walk along the same path or do you make new pathways for your career?

- Take five minutes to think about some of the things you would like to achieve in your sport—play at certain level, play for certain team, win trophies, travel or play against world's best.
- Now, think about all the things in your career you will be missing if you don't change some of your thoughts and feelings that are holding you back.
- Write down what you would be missing out on.
- What has having certain negative, limiting beliefs or negative behaviour, and putting things off cost you. Has it caused you pain in your career, affected your playing ability, affected your life?

As you stand at the crossroad, you can see that each side leads to different paths, journeys, and destinations.

As you look to the left, you see a slow, downward road. It is easy to take this "low road." You could just coast down it. It is the path of doing what you have always done. By continuing on that road you will keep getting what you have always got.

As you look to the right, you see a road that travels upward. It will take some effort to take this "high road." But, the road on the right is the way of freedom, choice, and life. It is the road of being in control of your sports career and life. It is the High Road to Success! It is the road you have decided to take by going for dreams, changing any negative behaviour, and being the best you can be.

> If you keep doing what you have always done in life, you will keep getting same results. If you want to change certain things in your life, you need to change what you are doing.

Look again at the road on the left. If you take this road, you will be carrying all of the negative feelings associated with continuing to put things off, carrying on living with limiting beliefs, and negative behaviours. If you choose this road, think of how you will be losing out in different aspects of your sports career and life, in your relationships with teammates, coaches, your abilities, and your sense of purpose. Really allow yourself to feel the burden of these self-destructive behaviours. Feel your desire to be free from all of the ill effects of hurting yourself with any negative and limiting beliefs.

Visualise travelling down that low road and living with those limitations one more year. Notice how after one year of not making any changes what your life is like. What have you missed out on because you have continued to do the same things?

What opportunities will you have missed out on a year from now? What will do be doing with your career? At what level will you be playing? Which team will you be playing for? Will you be happy?

Imagine looking into a mirror and asking yourself, "Am I pleased with myself after this year of participating in my sport and life the same way? Am I happy to have another year of carrying on doing the same things, thoughts, and limitations? Do I feel better having made this decision to carry on? Do I feel any disappointment continuing to not realise my potential in my sport for another year?

Travel down the low road for 5 more years and write down where you expect to be in your sport. At what level will you be playing, on which team will you be playing, has your ability changed, has your life changed by carrying on the same path?

Let's look forward another 10 years. What do you expect your sports career to be? Where will you be? What will you be doing? How will participating in your sport in the same way affect your life?

Finally, imagine you have reached the end of your playing or coaching career with the same attitude, application, desire, confidence, and motivation exactly as you are now.

What have you left behind? Have you made an impact on the lives of others? What legacy have you left? What are your achievements? What are some of the things you accomplished in sports? What are some of the things you wished you had done in sports? What are the thoughts of friends, family, teammates, fans, and coaches about you?

Go back and stand once again at the crossroad. This time, turn to the right and take the High Road.

Imagine taking the initiative and pursuing some of your goals in your sport, releasing the negative emotions and limiting beliefs that are stopping you from going forward.

Think about how different your sports career will be. At what level will you play, what team you will play for, will your ability have changed? What competitions and trophies will you have won?

If you take the high road, in a year from now what opportunities will you have created for you and other people? What is your sense of purpose in your career? How has your sports career changed? What is it like to be playing up to your potential?

Look into that mirror again and ask yourself, "Am I pleased with myself for making these positive choices? Would I ever go back to restraining my career by living with limitations? Am I glad that I have made these permanent changes?"

Look forward 5 more years on this high road. What will your sports career be like? At what level will you be playing? For which team will you play? How will your ability have changed? Which competitions and trophies will you have won?

In 5 years from now, what opportunities have you created for yourself and other people? What is your sense of purpose in your sports career? What its like to be playing up to your potential?

Focus on the 10-year point on this High Road of Success. There you are making good and positive changes in your mindset in your sport. Really allow yourself to feel the effects of these decisions of continuing to follow this new positive path.

By the end of your career, by taking the High Road, you have fulfilled your potential as a sports person. Enjoy the feeling of knowing that you have made a permanent change. Be grateful you did not go back to your old ways.

By following the High Road, what did you leave behind? What effect did you have on the lives of others? What is your legacy? What are your achievements? What are some of the things you accomplished in your sport? What are some of the things you wished you had accomplished in your sport? What are the thoughts of friends, family, teammates, fans, and coaches about you?

Follow the high road and limiting and negative beliefs about yourself will be a thing of the past. You will not make the mistake of allowing yourself to be bound by limitations now that you are free from negativity.

You will remain free for the rest of your life.

Conclusion

Modern sports have become a highly pressurised environment; many athletes seek to gain that "extra edge" over the opposition. This book contains information about the latest cutting-edge advancements in sports science to assist you with your fitness, technology, tactics, and techniques continue to be refined.

Psychology has played a big part in sports over the past ten years. You only have to listen to some of the top sports people in the world during press conferences and interviews to realise they have adapted a psychological process to assist with their success.

NLP has grown and will continue to grow because of its user friendliness and practicality in sports.

Success in sports is a matter of minute degrees. What separates the world's best performers from an average performer can be as little as a split second. The split second may come down to some focus, direction, or confidence. Ultimately, the measure of every successful athlete or performer is if they achieve their full potential. Whether you aspire to be the world's best or the best you can be, I wish you every success on your journey to excelling at sports.

About the Author

Jimmy Petruzzi is a world-renowned performance coach and NLP Expert. For more than 15 years he has worked with many top professional soccer teams and individuals at the national and international level in the English premiership and worldwide. He also works with international and Olympic athletes and top, professional sports people, helping them to achieve peak performance in all aspects of their lives. He is a consultant to several sports organisations and associations. Over the past 15 years, Jim has worked with thousands of people world-wide and is a sought after and highly regarded speaker for international conferences and seminars.

Jimmy is a regular columnist for several leading publications, including "Peak Performance" and "Men's Fitness," and appears regularly on television news and sports-related documentaries, on radio and in the press.

He is co-founder of the NLP Centre of Excellence ltd at www.excelwithnlp.com.

He won the Highly Commended Award for Coaching International and Domestic Work in 2006 and was nominated for Britain's top coach 2008.

If you wish to enquire about any courses, contact Jimmy Petruzzi at 0044 78180 32622 or at www.excelwithnlp.com.

Other Books from

DragonRising Publishing

The Perfect Fit—Ed Grimshaw

Advanced Skills For Finding And Hiring The Ideal Candidate

Here is a thorough approach to making good recruitment decisions and avoiding costly mistakes by using NLP Neuro Linguistic Programming. Learn how to attract, interview and test candidates without incurring extra profiling costs. Discover if the candidate matches your organisation's culture to be
The Perfect Fit.

EFT & NLP—Dr Silvia Hartmann

Special Report

NLP & EFT is a special report by Dr Silvia Hartmann on how to use EFT Emotional Freedom Techniques for NLP Practitioners. It covers how to use EFT to enhance NLP abilities in the self, how to use NLP skills and techniques to lift and expedite EFT sessions and NLP techniques. Includes additional information and special patterns for use with NLP and EFT in conjunction."

EmoTrance—Dr Silvia Hartmann

Patterns & Techniques of EmoTrance, Vol 1: Oceans of Energy

This book reveals one of the most important things you can ever learn about how to keep mentally and emotionally secure. Developed by Dr Hartmann after intensive personal research into how our bodies work and knowlege built on a foundation through her study of NLP, *Project Sanctuary*, and Emotional Freedom Techniques EFT, she has taken the revolutionary new field of energy therapy to the next level. Once the EmoTrance technique is mastered, it is possible to deal with any issue that may arise painlessly and effectively. As issues are dealt with one by one, one emerges into a world of health and vigor, where the world is filled with energy and life.

Adventures in EFT—Dr Silvia Hartmann

Learn and understand EFT with this practical and information packed manual that includes the A–Z of EFT techniques and how to use them with a wide variety of problems. Treat yourself for sadness, anger, addictions, low self esteem and a whole lot more! *Adventures In EFT* is the world's best selling guide for beginners in Gary Craig's Emotional Freedom Techniques EFT.

Project Sanctuary—Dr Silvia Hartmann

Project Sanctuary is a unique set of processes using intention, energy and metaphor. Developed by Dr Hartmann in 1993, it helps to heal the divide between the conscious mind and the energy mind. It is a fantastic, exciting and delightful process that every human being can engage in. "If you only buy ONE book in this lifetime— make it *Project Sanctuary*."

The Genius Symbols—Silvia Hartmann

Second Edition

Those who believe that they will never be a visionary genius just need to relearn how to think, says author Silvia Hartmann. *The Genius Symbols* are the ultimate tools for putting us directly in touch with our subconscious energy minds, so that we may ask direct questions and receive controlled answers. This book is the recommended starting point for anyone wishing to learn Project Sanctuary.

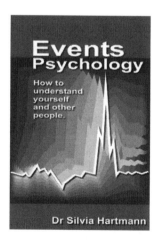

Events Psychology—Dr Silvia Hartmann

Dr Silvia Hartmann PhD, already famed for her work on EFT, EmoTrance, *Project Sanctuary* and *The Genius Symbols*, has discovered core principles of human psychology which finally answer questions about who we are, and ultimately, how we can become the best we can be without our own personal limitations. This research is called *Events Psychology* and is the next step for the field of psychology of understanding ourselves and other people.

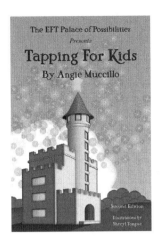

Tapping for Kids—Angie Muccillo

A Children's Guide To EFT Emotional Freedom Techniques

Tapping For Kids is an EFT children's book designed to teach 7–11-year-olds how to use EFT as a tool to help them overcome their fears, worries and everyday traumas, as well as build their self-esteem. *Tapping For Kids* is a perfect gift for all the children in your life!

Brand New, Full Colour Edition With Free Audio CD!

Tapping for Kids is now in its second, full-colour edition that brings the story to life and captures children's imagination whilst they learn EFT. In addition, *Tapping for Kids* now comes with a audio CD that is not available anywhere else. It is packed full of read-along raps and rhymes to help your child learn. You'll also be given a link to download posters and certificates to make the experience unforgettable.

The second edition paperback is now available for immediate release!

Power Affirmations—Dr Silvia Hartmann
Special Report

In this powerful, brand new, and highly focused 12-part, self-training program, Dr Silvia Hartmann explains precisely and concisely how you can make affirmations that work exactly like magic spells to create YOUR reality of choice. From strikingly simple exercises for absolute beginners to the amazing Super Magic Affirmations and the Vega Pattern at the other end of the scale, this concise treatise will give you the tools to make affirmations finally come to life and really start to WORK FOR YOU!